Let's Talk

Let's Talk

Eleven Conversations for People Who Take Life,
Faith, and the Church Seriously

DAVID BLANCHARD

RESOURCE *Publications* • Eugene, Oregon

LET'S TALK
Eleven Conversations for People Who Take Life, Faith, and the Church
Seriously

Resource Publications
An Imprint of Wipf and Stock Publishers
199 W. 8th Ave., Suite 3
Eugene, OR 97401

www.wipfandstock.com

PAPERBACK ISBN: 979-8-3852-1390-0
HARDCOVER ISBN: 979-8-3852-1391-7
EBOOK ISBN: 979-8-3852-1392-4

02/27/24

Contents

Contents

Preface

YOU DON'T HAVE TO like this book. You don't need to agree with me on every subject and you probably shouldn't anyway. The intention of this book is to spark necessary conversations among people who are seeking Jesus. For the longtime Christ follower, this book is designed to challenge some of your thinking and practices just enough to keep you honest. For novices and beginners, the aim is to provide alternative viewpoints to some you likely encounter in mainstream evangelical circles. For those who are seeking Jesus, but still don't know what to think about Christianity, I hope these pages convey the raw authenticity that you and I both seek among God's people. Lastly, for those who like the idea of Jesus but don't love organized religion, those who have tried church and been neglected, wounded, or ostracized in some way, I pray you find a friend in this book who sees you and identifies in many ways with your experiences. You are not alone. God loves you. His church needs you.

This book is written for the individual who enjoys reading and reflecting on topics of a spiritual nature, particularly those involving discipleship and the Christian church in her various shapes and sizes. This book is also written for people to use as a conversation starter in small group settings. Discussion questions accompany each of these chapters for use in personal reflection and as prompts for group conversation. The goal of this book is to get people talking about topics that (should) matter to people who are serious about their daily walk with Jesus and his people.

Introduction

YEARS AGO, I ARGUED with a youth group parent who believed intramural soccer was more important for her son than involvement with our student ministry. When schedules conflicted between our programs, this parent prioritized soccer matches over youth group every time. Youth workers will not be surprised here. These are the priorities of most parents and teens in our ministry programs.

On one occasion a late-night soccer match resulted in this teenager missing a group Bible study the next morning. Days later I approached his (slightly intimidating) mother to share my concerns about her son missing youth group. (Yes, I was young, idealistic, and foolish in my early years as a student minister.) What this parent said has stuck with me for over twenty years. It stung then, and it stings now. I don't remember the entirety of her statement, but I will never forget her opening line.

"Listen. I know soccer might not get him to heaven, but . . ."

I couldn't believe my ears. Did she hear what she just said? This parent claimed to know the difference between things that would lead her son to heaven or not, and she unapologetically chose something that "might not get him to heaven" as more important than something else that might. What?!

I've grown a lot since that conversation. I no longer see high school soccer games and weekly youth group gatherings as diametrically opposed, nor do I think God is any more or less at work in either setting. I do still believe that my youth group parent held to this thinking all those years ago. She believed it was either soccer or heaven for her son—and she chose soccer.

"It might not get him to heaven, but . . ."

Ever since that conversation I've promised myself that if I ever wrote a book, that interaction would absolutely be included. Now I've written a book. Now I've made good on my promise.

This book is dedicated to that youth group mom—a good person, who loved Jesus in her own way, and whose soccer-playing son eventually became a youth minister. Praise be to God.

1. The Honest Truth

PEOPLE COMPLIMENT ME FOR being honest. I never know what to think about this. Shouldn't everyone be honest? Isn't this our expectation of decent people across the board? Apparently not.

This book is honest. You may disagree with the content. I may be way off in my thinking and assessments. I don't have all the answers, and I am often wrong about a good number of things. Honesty is not always accuracy. If nothing else, honesty is authenticity in its fullest.

Disclaimers aside, let's get right to it. Have you ever heard (or used) the following phrases?

"If I'm being honest . . ."

"To be perfectly honest with you . . ."

"If I'm *really* honest, then . . ."

What do these statements even mean? What do we think when someone pauses a flowing dialogue to make sure everyone knows they are about to say something that is *honest*? Does this mean everything else they have said, and will resume saying after the "honest" bit, is a lie? It seems to me that truly honest people should never need this qualifier in their interactions with others. I don't trust people who regularly differentiate between the "honest" parts of what they share and everything else that comes out of their mouth. You should expect me to be an honest person, and I certainly expect this of you in return. We do well to eliminate these qualifiers from our conversations.

The reality is that honesty makes us uncomfortable. Has anyone ever asked you if their outfit made them look fat? If you like their new haircut? If you are a fan of the Beatles? In the case of clothes and hairstyles, we know intuitively that honesty may *not* be the best policy! As an honest person, I struggle with this deeply. I don't want to lie to you, especially if you have asked for my *honest* opinion. At the same time, if your haircut looks terrible, if your new baby is ugly, or if your tacos needed more seasoning, I'm not sure how to *honestly* respond when you ask me about such things. There is often something good to say, and I try to find the good in each of these circumstances. "Hey! You've changed your look. I bet that haircut feels great!" Does this sound dishonest? I feel like it is. That said, I also don't want to hurt someone because I personally dislike their hairstyle. This is a simple example. Overweight people and parents of ugly babies need to stop asking other people about their issues altogether. These matters present a whole new degree of difficulty in the "speaking honestly without hurting people" department. If you suspect you look fat in your outfit, do the rest of us a favor and stop asking for a second opinion. Babies are off limits entirely. Your baby is beautiful in your eyes. The end.

Taco seasoning is a slightly different issue. I will never offer my opinion that your tacos were bland. But if you ask? This requires some discernment. Seasoning is a preferential matter, and your preference may be very different than mine. "Wait a minute," you say, "hairstyles are also a preferential matter. How dare you determine my haircut looks bad when that is also merely your opinion?" Fair enough. But here's a little exercise to consider. What if I tell you that I don't like the Beatles? (I can feel the collective gasp of almost all seven people who will ever read this book.) The cultural narrative surrounding pop culture in North America *demands* that I like the Beatles. We *all* like the Beatles, don't we? We *all* love *The Princess Bride*. We *all* enjoy the game of baseball. Nope. Some of us do not. To be honest is to say so when asked. I won't offer my opinion on your hairstyle or taco seasoning—unless you ask. Furthermore, I am entitled to my own opinion when we differ in our cultural preferences. You don't have to like my movies, music, or favorite restaurants—and I don't have to like yours. Quit trying to convince me that kombucha is any good or that goat yoga has any merit for sane people. We can be honest with one another, respectfully. We can disagree.

As I see it, there are two keys to honest conversation. These should be common sense, but it seems we need a refresher. First, be honest *when asked*. There are times for honest people to interject, to make public statements, to speak prophetically, with conviction, even when others have not asked them to do so. You have encountered people like these on occasion. They may have rubbed you wrong or made you uncomfortable. Such were the prophets of the Bible and often the poets of popular culture. Poets (songwriters, authors, scriptwriters, artists) fare better in the public eye. Prophets are berated, cast out, and executed. Be prophetic when you must but expect consequences. Our world desperately needs people of conviction that will stand up to intolerance and injustice, people who will make a public stand for causes more important than the comfort of keeping their mouths shut and their opinions to themselves. Honest conversation sometimes means uncomfortable, unpopular, and unwelcome viewpoints. I encourage you to speak (thoughtfully, carefully) into things that matter. Speak boldly, clearly, with conviction. On almost everything else, it's best to keep your mouth shut. Keep it to yourself unless someone asks you to share. Sorry to say so. *I'm just being honest.*

Second, when asking others their views and opinions, *expect* them to be honest in their replies. Don't tolerate the yes-man; don't suffer the politician. Press others if you see through their facade. Find new friends if necessary. *Dishonest* people abound. Here's the deal: you don't have to agree with me or even like my opinion, but if you ask what I think, you owe me the opportunity to provide an honest response. I'm assuming because *you have asked* how I feel about this or that you honestly want to know how I honestly feel in return. If you aren't seeking honesty, then don't bother asking. This seems simple enough to me. Your tacos were bland. I wasn't planning to say anything about this, but you asked for my—wait for it—*honest* opinion. Don't be hurt or offended. Be thankful you have at least one person in your life who will tell you the truth. Most people will not. Some of those people are talking behind your back about the blandness of your tacos. You know this is true because you've done it yourself.

I offer this little book as an honest reflection and assessment of a few things from my own experience in life and ministry that need some attention. I realize the irony here. None of you have asked my opinion about anything in these pages. I am breaking rule number one above. I do think, however, that you are an intelligent person, capable of choosing what to read and from whom. If you've made it this far and choose to continue forward, this is basically the same thing as asking my opinion on all that you find in the pages to come. Again, you don't have to *agree* with me on anything you find here. I do ask that you consent to the rules above as a contract of sorts throughout our time together. Choosing to read is asking me to speak honestly. I expect you to be honest in return and look forward to hearing from *some* of you when you've finished the book. Notice how I was honest there? I doubt any writer has been thrilled by every response to or assessment of their work. Church work has taught me that stinkers are often the ones with the loudest voices. Be honest with me, but don't be a stinker. Most of what follows has something to do with Jesus, I think. At least this is my intention. I have plenty to say about the church— I write this book for you. Because of you. Despite you. I'm also "coming out" in my own way here, I suppose. After twenty-some years in paid ministry roles, it's time I present my own *honest* self to the public. So, here's the big reveal, right out of the gate . . .

DISCUSSION 1

Text—Matthew 5:37; Ephesians 4:25; James 5:12

1. Be honest. Are you in the habit of using "honesty qualifiers" when speaking with others? If so, why do you feel a need to tell someone when you are being honest?

2. Describe some scenarios in which speaking honestly is particularly difficult. Why is speaking honestly more challenging in these situations?

3. Is it fair to expect honesty from all parties, always, as a fundamental requirement of healthy interpersonal communication? Is this an appropriate standard for Christ followers, in particular? Explain.

4. Matthew 5:37 comes from a teaching about oath-giving (verses 33–37). Is there a principle here that applies to speaking honestly on all occasions? Explain. How does this passage compare to James 5:12?

5. What is your experience of other Christians when it comes to speaking honestly with others? Is it fair to expect a higher standard from God's people?

6. Ephesians 4:25 comes from a chapter devoted to Christian unity. Is it possible for groups of Christians to be united when a culture of dishonesty is alive and well in their midst?

7. Imagine a church in which people smile and exchange pleasantries, but rarely speak truth. Imagine a community of Christ followers in which honest interactions are few and far between. Describe this church. Have you been here before?

2. Confessions

I AM A FAN of eighties metal music. There it is. Judge me however you like. As a child of the eighties, the soundtrack to my childhood includes some of the best music ever made. Van Halen, Bon Jovi, Def Leppard—bands with big hair and one-armed drummers. Name a metal band from this era, and there's a good chance they are in my personal playlist. I've read memoirs from Sammy Hagar and Dee Snider. I watch documentaries about music from this era. I eat it up. Hear my confession.

I am also a big fan of nineties grunge music. This was the soundtrack of my teenage years, clothed in flannel and full of angst. Nirvana, Pearl Jam, Alice in Chains—bands with edgy melodies, interesting vocals, and suitcases of illegal drugs in their dressing rooms. These are all in my playlist as well. As with my eighties metal obsession, I explore all media related to this genre. One of the best books I've read this past year is a new release from Dave Grohl. This one touched me deeply enough that I wrote him a personal letter when I finished. (I'm still waiting for a reply.) Hear my confession.

Now, for the big one. My final confession (for now). I've never been a fan of contemporary Christian music. I don't listen to this ever, really. I don't particularly like it. Now, just relax; settle down and give me a chance here. Yes, I have been a professional (paid) minister for over twenty years. Yes, I love Jesus. Yes, I think there are some incredible arrangements in this genre, many with deep and rich messages that encourage believers and bring glory to

God. When it comes to the music I prefer for my playlist, this is one category I typically exclude. Hear my confession.

Which is worse? An affinity for secular and "worldly" music, or a dislike for the Christian music commonly found on your local radio station? I could argue this both ways. Some of the deepest and most spiritual messages are found in music you might not suspect. (Ever heard of U2?) To my ears, Van Halen's "Judgment Day" is a call for people to get right with Jesus—lyrics I have used in teaching about repentance and baptism. Nirvana's "Jesus Doesn't Want Me for a Sunbeam" is ripe for discussion among Christians who are timid and self-defeated, living in perpetual guilt for not being "good enough" to ever do anything worthwhile for the kingdom. Even AC/DC presents a cautionary message in their "Highway to Hell," naming the desires of our self-indulgent, personal-pleasures-at-all-costs society. Their intent is to celebrate this lifestyle; my ears hear prophets who recognize the common desires of many human hearts. Ugh. This is one song I flip past when it pops up in the shuffle. It is true. It hurts.

Now to the question you may be asking. How does a committed Christian husband and father, a leader and teacher of others, and long-time professional minister, arrive at this odd place with his musical interests and sensibilities? It's a common assumption that people with my profile have more Chris Tomlin than Iron Maiden in their personal playlist. This is an assumption, indeed.

I love the churches who have nurtured my faith from infancy to young adulthood. I have great affinity for my tribe (denomination). Ours is a tradition of a cappella (voices only, no instruments) worship. Our music is rich and beautiful—the only way it works is with full participation from everyone in the assembly. We sing in four-part harmony, and without instrumentation; we hear all the voices clearly. Our singing is awesome, and our shared experience is beautiful. I love this about my tribe.

I also realize this is a foreign worship style to many, and I understand this tradition is odd to those from other tribes. After all, why not have an organ or guitar? People of my age, from churches like mine, will know what it's like to be the odd one out among your Christian friends in this regard—trying to explain and defend this tradition, because it is the one issue everyone wants to discuss when they learn of your practice. We are the weirdos. To be fair, in its extreme expressions, ours is an anti-instrument tradition. This is a little weird. (Just being honest.)

My tribe rejects instruments based on our method of biblical interpretation. Historically, my people are part of a Restoration Movement aspiring to "restore" the life and practice of contemporary churches to the forms and functions found in the pages of our New Testament. We look diligently for patterns and prescriptions; we identify commands from New Testament writers and uphold examples of early practice as our standards in matters of Christian life and corporate worship. Because Paul speaks of psalms, hymns, and spiritual songs in his letters to the Ephesians and Colossians—because voices are mandatory here and instruments not mentioned explicitly—our people have traditionally interpreted instrumental music to be excluded (by God, via Paul) from corporate worship gatherings. "If God wanted instruments in our worship, God would have communicated this specifically through Paul in these letters." Make sense? You don't have to agree with any of this. Just try to get your head around it so I can make my point. Moving on . . .

Here's where the thinking and practice of my people becomes (more) confusing. Because of our traditional view of instruments as sinful in worship settings, some have rejected the contemporary Christian industry as misguided and unpleasing to God. For worship to be right and acceptable, whether in an auditorium or on your car radio, it must be with voices only (a cappella). Please understand, not all the churches in our tribe go this far—I just happen to come from some churches like these, myself. Believe it or not, these churches are still out there. I know—weird, huh? Back to my point. Because instruments were viewed as sinful in worship music, kids like me were dissuaded from listening to "Christian" music on the radio. So what did we listen to instead?

This is a great example of how bizarre the thinking can be in our churches, even with the absolute best of intentions. For kids like me, it was better to listen to Ozzy Osborne than to Michael W. Smith. Ozzy was in no way a Christian artist or role model, but at least he wasn't producing "Christian" music with instrumentation. Weighed in the balance, Ozzy was preferable for your personal playlist. The difference here is subtle, but important. Ozzy doesn't aspire to honor God. "Christian" music, presented improperly (with instruments), absolutely dishonors God—all in the name of glory and adoration. To a kid like me, this was the clear message from our platforms and pulpits.

Throughout my childhood and teenage years, I developed an affinity for the music of our secular culture, otherwise known as "normal music" to most people. I've always loved the guitars and drums; I like the volume, the reverberation. I can do without the lifestyles promoted in these circles, but I do appreciate the authenticity of many of these songwriters. The hair and spandex, the torn jeans and Doc Martens—these were all part of an act, expressions of young people dissociating from the Establishment. That said, the lyrical messages were often more honest than what many of us heard from teachers, politicians, and sometimes even our pastors. There never would have been a Rage Against the Machine if the machine hadn't incited rage in the first place. This was nothing new in the eighties or nineties—go back and listen to some Creedence.

As for the scene in contemporary Christian music, I certainly have my opinions. My views have evolved over the years. No longer do I ascribe to the teaching that instruments are sinful in a worship setting. I don't think there's anything wrong with Christian contemporary music that relates to the instrumentation. If your playlist is full of Mercy Me and Elevation Worship, I have no problem with this. If your church wants a band, an organ, or a bell choir—knock yourselves out. I don't share the concerns of the churches that raised me. My uneasiness with this genre stems from other matters.

I've been to a Hillsong church. As you might expect, the music was excellent. Well-rehearsed, well-played, well-presented. The talent level of these musicians was on par with any professional music group, and the experience was just as electric as any metal concert I've attended over the years. I totally understood the draw to this church; it made perfect sense to me that young, creative, and expressive people waited together in a long line before the doors to this venue opened. There was a buzz, an eagerness, an expectation for the multisensory experience about to occur. What followed for me was a worship experience I will never forget. Hillsong worship is quite different from the worship of my childhood. Closer to Freddy Mercury than Fanny Crosby.

When worship concluded at Hillsong and the crowd headed for the doors, we were funneled past tables (yes, multiple) of music and merchandise that are sold at this venue every Sunday. Stacks of CDs, T-shirts, hats—all the things I've seen at Metallica concerts in the past. I don't know if there was an autograph session, but I would not be surprised had there been.

For me, this is troublesome. At what point does a worship experience become a concert? Furthermore, when (if ever) is it appropriate to promote concerts, with their productions, performers, and proliferation of assorted merchandise in the name of Christian worship. I fear our worship may sometimes be misplaced. Who and what we worship as mediated by how and where we worship. All this becomes convoluted at some point if we aren't careful.

I know, I sound like a grumpy old codger. Nevertheless, these are fair questions that deserve attention. I'm sure there were others around me who experienced something worshipful that night at Hillsong. Praise God for this. What I experienced was a full-blown concert, complete with professional lighting, fog machines, digital displays, beautiful and charismatic people in black leather with the "it-factor" of any celebrity—and multiple tables of merch I was encouraged to buy before exiting the venue. If God is glorified through all this, then I am all for it. We need more worship, not less. Maybe I'm just not a Hillsong guy.

But I have been a professional pastor. I've seen behind the curtain. I've sat in staff meetings with my own people where we discussed the "production value" of what we would put on stage the next Sunday morning. True story. Someone actually used those words as our staff discussed things like lighting, volume, and the need for expensive additions to our audio-video capabilities. This particular church had "gone instrumental" by jettisoning our a capella heritage in favor of something "more relevant" to the surrounding community. We spent hundreds of thousands of dollars on staff additions, acoustic treatments, soundboards, audio-video upgrades, and yes, the requisite instrumentation to enable our weekly "production." The goal was to provide an experience for visitors that would keep them coming back, enabling our church to grow numerically. I didn't last long at this church.

My distaste for contemporary Christian music has more to do with my upbringing than my experiences as an adult. I was raised by good, God-fearing people who inadvertently steered me to Ozzy. Let me be clear, I have nothing against the Christian music genre—I am thankful for artists who encourage others and bring glory to God. Praise God for this. I do have something against the commodification and monetization of "worship" for those who stand to profit for personal and institutional gain. Experiencing worship as a concert-like experience is one thing. Providing a concert to pad our church numbers or make a buck at the merchandise table is a different thing altogether. One of these things occurs to glorify God, the other tends toward glorification of performers and staff meetings where "production value" is more important than nurturing a community to follow Jesus with the whole of their lives.

I expect all the bands in my secular playlist to provide top-notch productions at their respective venues. I have no desire of this from my church. If I want a concert, I will choose Van Halen every time. If I want to worship, I can do this with or without instruments. With or without a stage, light show, or trendy front man/woman whose poster I can buy in the foyer. Hear my confession.

DISCUSSION 2

Text—Micah 6:6–8; Romans 12:1–2; Colossians 3:15–17

1. What are some of your favorite bands? Why are these your favorites?

2. What is your initial reaction to this chapter? Where do you find agreement with the author, if at all? With which portions do you disagree? Is the author crazy? Hypocritical? Explain.

3. Worship is a deeply personal matter. People hold strong opinions about the musical expressions of corporate worship, in particular. Why is this aspect of our worship so emotionally charged within and among different Christian traditions?

4. Read the passages from Mic 6 and Rom 12. What can we learn here about the time and place, the heart and motive of deep and authentic expressions of worship? How well do we understand, teach, and practice these principles in our personal lives? In our churches?

5. Colossians 3:15–17 is cited by some as a prescriptive teaching for how corporate worship should function when God's people gather (Eph 5:19–20 cited similarly). If this is true, how do these pictures compare to our typical worship assemblies today? What have we added? What are we missing?

6. Is there a line that separates authentic worshipful expression from consumer-driven offerings and performances? If so, what is that line? In your opinion, is there anything wrong with living on one side or the other? Is "crossing the line" an issue that deserves our attention at all?

7. Imagine a church in which worship is practiced in its fullness, by all parties, always. What would a corporate worship gathering look and feel like here? How similar would this experience be to worship gatherings with which you have participated in the past?

3. Crosses

I RECENTLY FOUND AN opportunity for theological reflection at my local Panda Express. It's amazing how the Spirit works, presenting things to us in the most unlikely of circumstances—if only we will look and listen attentively. I believe this was one such experience.

There I was, standing in line, craning my neck to see past the other customers, trying to see if the teriyaki chicken was over-charred again. As I looked over, past, and between the others in line, something else caught my eye. Immediately in front of me, a young family was basically doing the same thing as they waited their turn. This was a cute family, a younger couple with a little boy, straining on his tiptoes to see if the teriyaki chicken was over-charred again. It was the father who got my attention. This young man wore a shiny silver necklace, a hefty chain adorned by a big silver cross.

I recognized this cross immediately. Some of you may have too (whether you admit it or not). This was the cross of Dominic Toretto. Fans of the *Fast and Furious* movies know this cross very well. Dominic (Dom) receives, gives, loses, displays, and wears this cross at various times throughout this ten-movies-and-counting cinematic masterpiece (don't judge me, haters). Dom is known by his cross as much as he is for his garage, his cars, and his love for family. This cross—Dom's cross—is an important part of the narrative continuity that holds these movies together. As icons go, this cross would serve as a visual representation of the story that continues to unfold every year or two in our theaters.

As a fan of the *Fast and Furious* movies, I was interested to see this movie-quality replica hanging on the neck of some guy at Panda Express. I smiled to myself as I examined his cross—Dom's cross—and wondered if he knew the significance of his jewelry. I was just about to ask my fellow line-stander if he was a fan, if he had also seen all the movies, if he too aspired to be like Dom one day, when my moment of theological reflection ensued.

There I was, intrigued by a cross hanging on the neck of a total stranger. I found common ground with this person immediately as I recognized the significance of his *particular* cross—Dom's cross. My impulse was to connect, to engage conversation; I wanted to know this guy better and have a conversation about our shared interests in fast cars and action movies. The sight of this cross stirred something within me, it triggered a social and emotional impulse I wanted to share.

Then it hit me. I wanted to share a moment of connection over a cross—Dom's cross—in which Hollywood, not holiness, would be the topic of our conversation. I saw that cross and immediately thought "Dom" without even considering Jesus. The one who hung on the cross to begin with. The reason crosses are anywhere to be found at all, these two thousand years later. I was intrigued by the cross of Dom in ways that I am often ambivalent to the cross of Christ. I chose not to engage. Instead, from that moment forward, I have been reflecting on this experience.

I'm not sure how I feel about all the crosses I encounter daily. Our family has moved more than I like to admit, and we have enjoyed a good deal of domestic travel; we have experienced firsthand a variety of subcultures across North America. I am quite aware there are more crosses in some places than others. The ubiquity of crosses in places like Oklahoma and Texas provides a stark contrast to what we have seen in Michigan and Pennsylvania. Some contexts adorn themselves, their cars, their homes, and their social media accounts more than others. As we settle into Colorado Springs, I am increasingly aware of the significant evangelical presence and the prevalence of crosses in our own community.

I want to say this is a good thing. I hope it is. We need to focus on the cross for all it represents, and we do well to remind ourselves and others regularly. The cross should be powerful—it should illicit a response when you and I see it. But in many places, I see crosses everywhere. I've seen crosses stitched into gun holsters (looking at you, Texas), stamped into metal flasks (whiskey for Jesus!), and wrapped in American flags. Maybe you haven't. What about bedazzled crosses on T-shirts, ball caps, and on the butt pockets of designer denim jeans? Have you encountered purses, wallets, belt buckles, boots, bandanas, bracelets, earrings, nose rings, hand rings, toe rings, or bumper stickers? If not, you haven't spent enough time in the South. What happens when the cultural proliferation of crosses blurs the lines between faith and fashion? Dom's cross is not Jesus' cross any more than the blinged-out butt pockets of some (hopefully well-intentioned) fashion designer. Crosses like these celebrate sales over Saviors.

Ouch. I know, one of the five people still reading this chapter is a sweet person, with a good heart, a strong faith, and a cross tattoo somewhere on their leg or forearm. It probably sounds like I'm being harsh. No, I don't wear crosses. I don't have a bumper sticker or even a Bible cover adorned by a cross. I could possibly do the tattoo thing, but not just yet. Hear me clearly. I am not belittling anyone who has, holds, or displays crosses like these on their person, car, home, or office. I'm not saying this is wrong, or that I think less of you. What I am saying is that we might all benefit from some deeper reflection on this issue.

The cross of Jesus—*the cross*—was a torture device designed to kill criminals. Our Savior was nailed to one. This was hard, rough wood, where an innocent man was affixed by large metal nails at his hands and feet. Jesus bled profusely here. This cross was covered in sweat and blood; it was stained by these, and it probably attracted flies long after the limp and lifeless body was removed. Dried blood, covered in flies, on a torture device that was used to murder our Lord and Savior. How should we think of this cross— *the cross*—the only cross that has ever mattered?

Not as an icon to represent a Hollywood movie franchise. Not as a fashion adornment to bling out the latest chic accessory. Not as a component piece to the Nashville souvenirs that combine Christianity, camouflage, NASCAR, and Jack Daniels whiskey into trinkets that sell to locals and tourists alike (I have seen all these incorporated together into murals on artwork, T-shirts, and souvenir coffee mugs—you can actually buy this stuff in Tennessee). Is this the best use of a cross—*the cross*—in our world today? Are any of these *appropriate* uses of crosses to the extent they represent *the cross* and the Godman who died a cruel death nailed to its timbers? If these crosses don't represent *the cross*, then let's admit what they are in the first place. Fashion statements. Tourist trinkets.

To the extent any of our cultural crosses represent *the cross*, we should probably consider more deeply the aesthetical (and commercial) interpretations of this death instrument. *The cross* was not bedazzled. *The cross* was not soft, fuzzy, or shiny; it is not presented accurately by flowing lines or with curly designs. We present crosses in these ways to make them fashionable. Artistic interpretations of the cross must be palatable for us to embrace their appeal; for us to endure the horror they represent when taken seriously. Crosses of these kind sell. No one wants a necklace adorned by a blinged-out electric chair. I doubt many want T-shirts with images of Christian martyrs burning on their respective stakes. Maybe we should imitate our Catholic friends here. Beyond sterilized and fashionable crosses, the traditional Catholic crucifix also displays the beaten and bloody body of Jesus. This focuses our attention differently. I see fewer of these where I live and travel. Bloody bodies are harder to sell to evangelical Christians.

The NIV translation of Gal 5:11 speaks of the cross as being *offensive*. In this context, Paul recognizes the challenge of accepting grace through Jesus Christ for those who are confused by the cross event. Jewish thinkers wrestled with interpretations of the crucifixion, many of whom assumed there was still need to follow their former laws to be right with God. To this audience, the cross was a stumbling block, a point of confusion, even an offensive reference to those who simply couldn't get their heads around salvation through Jesus Christ. I've always liked this translation. What if we stopped to consider all the ways in which the cross is *offensive*. God chose to die on such a cross. This cross—*the cross*—was a human invention; something we made, something we operated, something we celebrated then and carry around on our handbags now. Let's be perfectly clear. This cross—*the cross*—symbolizes the whole of humankind giving our all-powerful and creator God the middle finger. That should be offensive to all of us. How dare they? *How dare we?*

I am more interested in being branded *by* the cross than in making it my brand. The cross is offensive. Is that what you want on your bedazzled baseball cap? I know it's cute, and I understand it's in fashion. Plenty of great people wear these, people who love Jesus and represent him well with others. I'm thankful for each of them. Wear your necklace, get your tattoo, display your bumper sticker. The world needs to hear, and the church needs the encouragement. I'm not saying these things are wrong, and I'm not telling you to stop. I'm simply offering a different perspective. I cling to *the cross*. I'm forever thankful to our Savior who willingly died there for you and me and them and they and all the others who don't even care or want anything to do with it. Without Jesus there is no hope. Without Jesus there is no cross.

DISCUSSION 3

Text—Matthew 16:24–27; 1 Corinthians 1:18–25

1. Where have you most seen crosses displayed in your own cultural context? Have you encountered any that struck you as odd? (Have you ever considered this before?)

2. How do you feel about crosses as fashion accessories? Is there anything wrong with displaying crosses on hats, handbags, or gun holsters?

3. In Matt 16, Jesus instructs his followers to take up their crosses and follow him. Practically speaking, what does this mean for us today? Is there any correlation between "taking up our cross" and displaying a cross on our person?

4. How do you respond to the author's assessment of the cross as humanity's "middle finger" to God? This stings to read and feels almost inappropriate, somehow. Should the cross be conceived any other way?

5. Read 1 Cor 1:18–25. In what sense is the cross "foolishness" to those who are perishing? Conversely, how can the instrument used in the murder of Jesus be interpreted as the "power of God" to those who are being saved? Explain.

6. Notice the subjective interpretations of the cross as outlined in the passage above. How do you think most people interpret crosses they encounter on bumper stickers, belt buckles, and business signage today? Is there need for us to consider this issue more deeply, as our author suggests? What do you think?

7. Imagine a church in which the cross meant more than wall adornments or architectural statements. Imagine a group of Christians committed to taking up their crosses daily to follow Jesus in his expressions of love and self-sacrifice. How might this church function differently than others you have encountered?

4. Secrets

I ONCE KNEW A man who had cheated on his wife. I knew this because he told me. It's amazing the things people share when they learn you are a minister. In this case, I had known this person long enough to become friends. The confession was hard to hear, but I'm thankful he shared. Who knows if I handled this well. Receiving a confession can be as awkward as offering one.

I did my best to listen. I asked questions to better understand the situation. I tried to maintain a poker face, disallowing my inner turmoil from surfacing through facial expression or body language. This was someone who knew better; someone I respected. I did not see this coming. My goal that day was to extend grace and mercy. My desire was to affirm the goodness of a penitent heart and remind this person of the restoration found in Jesus. I think I did *that part* well. I think?

After much conversation, we came to the difficult part. I told my friend he needed to come clean with his wife. Confessing to me was a good start, but ultimately, I wasn't the person who needed to know. Pause here for a moment and imagine being in either of our shoes that day. As ministry goes, these are sacred ground moments—occasions in which God uses you to receive and restore others, in all the nasty messiness of life. These are also the gut-wrenching moments that can ruin your day, mess with your head, and bring deep sorrow to your heart. How could this happen? Why did this happen?

Sin. Plain and simple. Sin allures and intoxicates. Sin seduces and destroys. Sin holds a gravitational pull on our lives that tethers us through temptation and destroys us in moments of weakness. Sin has power that can overwhelm even the strongest of us all. As for the larger point I want to make today: *sin holds power in secrecy.*

My friend bristled at the idea of disclosing his infidelities to his wife. While he agreed this was necessary, he urged me to keep his secret "until the time was right" to share. Let me ask you: when exactly is the "right time" to share something like this with your spouse? Is there a magical moment for conversations like these? Do the planets align? Is there a specific restaurant in which to broach this topic? Maybe you save this for a vacation, an anniversary, or another special occasion? I suppose you could wait for your partner to do something stupid and become the guilty party for an offense of their own? As far as I can tell, the only "right time" to deal with conversations like these is right away. Why let things fester? Why continue to lie? Sin holds power in secrecy.

I told my friend his activities must stop immediately. I forbade him from sleeping with his wife (as though I could mandate this in any way at all) until he was tested for STDs. I agreed to keep the secret for a very short while, until he could be tested, and to allow him to disclose this information himself. What else was I supposed to do? Here's what I've learned since. Sin holds power in secrecy.

My friend eventually came clean with his wife. As things turned out, the time was never "right" to confess—he simply got caught in his sin. His secret was discovered. The secret that gave power to his sin. The illusion of a compartmentalized life in which marriage and affair were sustainable as long as no one ever found out. Both holy matrimony, and *holy crap, you did what, with whom, for how long?*

Sin holds power in secrecy. Power to convince us we will never be caught, power to ostracize us from others who might hold us accountable. Secrecy isolates and estranges us from others; often, from the very people who love and care enough about us to help—if only they knew what was happening behind the scenes.

Spouses, family, friends, coworkers, fellow church members. We keep our sins secret. Satan wants it this way. The longer our sins are secret, the more likely we are to believe we will never be caught. In cases like these, secret sin begets secret sins. If I can cheat on my wife with one person and get away with it, what's stopping me from cheating with two or three or twelve other people down the road? *Sin holds power in secrecy.*

Sometimes we empower the sins of others, keeping secrets on their behalf. In the case of my experience above, I kept the sins of a friend secret long enough for him to commit additional infidelities. More lives were affected; more people hurt when things finally came into light. Who knows what would have happened had I forced (facilitated?) a conversation between this person and his wife the day I learned of his secret sin? What if I had allowed him forty-eight hours to tell her? Situations like these are always unique, each with contextual details and nuance that call for careful discernment. While confessional grace periods may be important to certain situations, immediate action may be necessary for others. As a youth worker, I've been a mandated reporter for years. I've made more than one call to the authorities when situations merited immediate action. Sometimes lives are literally at stake.

I learned of a church recently that is wrestling with the strong probability of a sexual predator in their midst. Be assured that the leaders in this congregation are approaching this situation prayerfully, carefully, and with intentionality. The goal is to receive, restore, and appropriately restrict this person from serving in areas of ministry that involve young people. All of this, assuming the person in question comes clean of his formerly secret sins. Confession and repentance are necessary here. Admission of past (and current?) sins that have been harmful to others, and recognition that a formerly secret lifestyle must not ensue forward. Sin of this nature cannot be kept secret. Some sins hold greater power than others when it comes to their potential harm for others.

Years ago, I served a church that was sued by a former member who accused a volunteer of sexual misconduct. Supposedly, this person had been abused decades before, and was just now getting around to demanding justice. We never learned if these allegations were true. Too much time had passed, too many who were close to that situation had passed. Our insurance took care of all this without anyone going to court. But not before this hit the local newspaper.

I remember the meeting in which we discussed how to handle this allegation. I was the only person in the room with a young child at the time. My concern was for the kids and teenagers in our church. What if this person had abused a young person years ago and could possibly do this again? I argued strongly for limitations to be placed on this person, at least until we learned more. This person should not be allowed in or around our children's classrooms or in the bathrooms that flanked this portion of our building. This was prudent, in my opinion. This person should understand our concerns as a leadership and honor these parameters as appropriate, given our immediate circumstances.

I was alone with my opinion. The greater concern to my leaders was protecting the emotional health and public reputation of this man in question. *What?!* Hear me plainly, friends: this reasoning is exactly why perverts and predators find safe havens in our churches, private K-12s and Christian Universities. With the best of intentions, we don't want to "hurt" or embarrass people, so we find ourselves keeping secrets—sometimes incriminating secrets that hold potential to harm much more than the sinner in question. We would rather see children abused than abusers be embarrassed *by their own sinful behavior.* This is sick and wrong. I cannot state this strongly enough. We must stop empowering those with secret sins to sin further—especially when their sins are potentially (sexually, physically, emotionally) abusive to children, teenagers, and others disadvantaged by power in our churches and institutions. I'm not saying we tar and feather the offenders in our midst. I am saying we act with prudence as shepherds and stake holders in our respective communities.

The New Testament speaks of Jesus as the light of the world. Likewise, his church, his people, are called to be light bearers. Sin cannot exist in the light. Sin holds power in secrecy. Secrecy exists in the shadows; it thrives in darkness. Sin affects us all, and some of our sins hide deeper in the shadows than others. I'm not perfect and neither are you. We both have things in our past (and present?) for which we feel shame and regret. No one enjoys their sin becoming public, but this is very much our prescription for avoiding sins becoming *secret*. There's a reason confession and repentance are integral to the healthy and maturing lives of committed Christ followers. We simply cannot allow our sins to become secret—*sin holds power in secrecy*. We need the light to burn away the darkness. We need to come clean. We need to receive and encourage others who come clean with us. It goes both ways. We must repent and we must receive others who are penitent. Jesus offers restoration to you and me and we offer restoration to others on his behalf. Sin wants to become secret. Secret sin begets secret sins.

To those in leadership, those responsible for others in your small group, at your church, in your private Christian school: please take this all very seriously. People trust you to keep them safe. The people you serve don't always need to know all the dirty details of every sinner in their midst—a community that includes you and me and our spouses and children and friends. You are asked to exercise prayer and sound discernment, among a group of (hopefully) Godly people who are striving to honor him in all you say and do always and forever. It is your job to protect your flock. If this means sacrificing one public reputation to protect others' lives, so be it. Refuse to keep secrets that will give power to sin. Refuse to shelter sinners in communities where we don't ask or tell or *actually* care about the physical, emotional, or spiritual well-being of others. Shine the light on sin. Do whatever it takes to keep your people out of the darkness.

To those like me—people who occasionally receive a confession—may we exercise prayerful discernment to know how best to help our confessors. May we extend grace and mercy in ways that are healthy and appropriate. I pray the Holy Spirit will lead us to know when to listen and when to speak boldly. Maybe you are the catalyst to facilitate additional confessions to enable the possibility for healing and reconciliation among others. Maybe your confessor needs you to provide a gentle embrace; maybe they need you to provide a swift kick in the pants. You may need to do both things.

To everyone else: if I can offer one thing here, one admonition, one reminder of the truth of sin in a dark and fallen world, it is this. *Sin holds power in secrecy.* Avoid the temptation to keep your sins secret. Secret sin begets secret sins. Maybe you need to share a secret today. Maybe it's time you step out of the shadows and into the light. Restoration is possible—by the grace of Jesus—through repentance. Confess. Come clean. May our sins never become secret.

DISCUSSION 4

Text—Romans 6:1–14; Galatians 6:1–2; James 5:13–16;
1 John 1:5–10

1. What is it about secrecy that gives power to sin? Explain.

2. Paul speaks often about sin in his letter to the Romans (see 3:23 and 6:23 for why this topic is so important). Read Rom 6:1–14. Describe the relationship between baptized believers and their sins. Is a sinless life possible—even after pledging ourselves to Jesus?

3. Read the above passages from James and 1 John. What do these writers say about the role of confession in the lives of believers? To whom are we called to confess? For what purpose?

4. Have you ever confessed sin to another person? Have you ever received someone else's confession? Share a little about your experience. What prompted you to confess? How did you respond to your confessor?

5. Galatians 6:1–2 acknowledges the reality of sins that are not confessed and their potential for harm to the individuals and communities in which they fester. What principles do we find in this passage for addressing these sins appropriately?

6. What are some healthy parameters for groups of Christians committed to open sharing and personal accountability with otherwise secret sins? How do groups like these avoid abuses of power among their members? At what point do good intentions become cult-like practices?

7. Imagine a church in which sinners are embraced and restored. Imagine if this church refused to tolerate sin. Imagine if a culture existed here in which people confessed and received confessions of others as a regular part of their everyday walk together. Is a church of this kind even possible?

5. Exiles

IN THE WORLD OF outsiders, I am something of an insider. What follows is for my fellow exiles. I write for those who have often been forgotten and sometimes been forsaken by the very churches that claim to love them. I've been there, I've experienced this more than once, myself. I stand with you. I share your hurt and confusion. I too have been wounded by God's people. I have been exiled.

I write today at the request of a friend; someone I know well who has also been exiled. To the exiles who are reading, know that you matter and that you are not alone in your sometimes unfortunate experiences with God's people. Churches are full of imperfect people—including you and me, at one time or another. Some of us can hurt and estrange others without even trying. Odds are, there are at least a couple of stinkers in every church. You and I might even be the stinkers. This is all part of being human and flawed and beat up a bit through life's experiences. I don't think most stinkers wake up in the morning with the intention to stink. Stinking just happens sometimes. When we are on the receiving end; when we experience the stink of others—especially those in our churches who should know and live and talk and be better people by the grace of Jesus—this *really* stinks. Even more, it hurts.

I've dealt with stinkers for years. This is part of the job for anyone who serves in ministry, paid or volunteer. People can be the best and worst parts of our jobs; sometimes those are even the same people at different times of the day! (Yes, sometimes that person is me—I own this fully, and I really am *trying* to be more like Jesus.) I know this sounds harsh to some of you; I probably sound heartless and uncaring. To be clear, *most* of the people I've worked with in paid ministry have been awesome. But there's always a stinker or two in the mix. I love people as best I can. I don't always do this well. You can judge me a terrible person or unfit for ministry, but I promise you I am not alone among my colleagues. People work is hard. Jesus loved people better than anyone else in human history—and they killed him. God created the church as his agency to provide hope, healing, and home for people who are lost and afflicted—and the church, full of imperfect people (even stinkers) sometimes does more harm than good in his service.

I have been dismissed by two churches in my professional ministry career. I'm not allowed to share all the details—I was made to sign documents in both cases that prevent me from saying more. In one church I resigned as my impending termination drew near. In the other, I was simply fired. I had known this was common practice among some of our business-minded churches; I had known ministers who had experienced similar, and I had listened to their stories. "We are firing you. If you resign and pretend like this was your idea, we will pay you severance for a few months. If people learn you were fired, we owe you nothing." Sorry to break it to you friends, but this happens in our churches. In some of our congregations, this is standard operating procedure. Nothing personal, just business.

Welcome to exile. One day you have a place and a people, the next day you are removed and forgotten. This is exile of a certain kind. The kind I describe above can be slippery and sketchy; the stuff of backroom business dealings that have no place in our churches. I'm thankful this form of exile only exists for a particular subset of our larger exiled community (is community an oxymoron here?). I have a particular affinity for former ministers and missionaries who have been exiled through unfortunate (often undisclosed and sometimes unethical) experiences with their churches. I stand with you. You are not alone. We can talk whenever you like. Don't choose to be alone in your funk.

More broadly speaking, the exiles I have in mind today are those who once found a place and people in the church, but for whatever reason have dissociated from their ranks. Normal people. Wounded people. God's people—estranged by and from God's people. I've encountered many over the years who were church members in some way or another in their past but have become disillusioned through their *experience* of God's people. These are people who have chosen exile, some with good reason. I knew one man who refused to participate with his local church because of past experiences where "churches only cared about his money and that was all they ever talked about." One Sunday this man visited our church. Guess what the sermon was about that week? Yup. Back to exile he went. In fairness, this man didn't give our congregation much opportunity to challenge his preconceived ideas of churches as money hungry financial institutions. At the same time, this man is not alone in his *perception* of churches. There is a reason some churches gain this reputation. I've participated with more than one that puts a little *too much* emphasis on financial matters. I've heard the pleas, I've witnessed the campaigns, I'm aware of covenant commitments that outline expectations of gifts and tithes and donations. Churches sometimes emphasize financial matters to the detriment and neglect of others. I understand how this man came to his conclusions—regardless if they were accurate or even fair. His experiences were his experiences. I've experienced just enough of these to be sympathetic myself.

Some of you have chosen exile for similar reasons. You have dealt with a stinker or two; you've experienced pain and become disillusioned. People lied to you. People excluded you. People talked behind your back. People told you they didn't approve of your torn jeans at church on Sunday morning. People called you "family" at their church until your actual family was in need or you stopped attending the assemblies and suddenly, your "family" seemed to forget you ever existed at all. Somewhere along the way, you became tired of churches fighting about worship styles and gender roles and what version of the Bible to read and what types of media to consume and whether or not you could have a beer with your neighbor and what political party deserves your vote. You realized at some point that you love Jesus but can't afford to be vulnerable among his people. Jesus loves you too, but his people have often brought you pain. This is a common lament among exiles.

Some of you have experienced churches where strong personalities or family clans wield unhealthy power and influence. Others know churches where the largest donors hold the most sway. Many of us have experienced glaring deficiencies, sometimes even gross moral failures among church leaders. Some of us have experienced abuse. Some of you were driven into exile by people you trusted who took advantage of you in some form or fashion. Churches are not immune to these things. There are categories worse than "stinker" for the abusers among us. God will deal with them.

For these reasons and more, exile is a preferable option to many than involvement with God's people through a localized gathering of believers. Exiles can be "spiritual but not religious" or in love with Jesus without need for his church. I totally get it. For those who resonate with anything I have said so far—I stand with you. You are not alone. Your experiences were crappy, and I am sorry for them. Some of these things were nasty, wrong, and downright sinful. I am so, so sorry. Jesus still loves you, and so should his church. (And so should I.)

To be exiled is to live alone, without a place or people. To be a Christian in exile is an oxymoron. One cannot fully experience God's call for their life without a tangible, flesh and blood community of believers with whom to laugh, and eat, and play, and serve, and worship, and celebrate everything from birth to baptism to marriage and to death. The church was created to be a community of people living in relationship with God and each other, to provide an alternative experience of life and meaning and mission that allows all people to experience God's kingdom in a limited sense on this side of heaven. You and I hold the potential for others to see and experience and know God better—through their experience of us, through our mutual experience of one another. Without you, I miss an opportunity to learn more about the Spirit within you and the God whose image you bear. Without me, you miss this as well. Christians were never intended to live this life in isolation—disillusioned, dissociated, or exiled from the church, the very *bride* of Christ. We are designed to have a people, to *be* a people. We are meant to have a place. I don't care if your place is an auditorium, a classroom, a living room, or a neighborhood pub. The point is less about a physical location and more about a psychosocial, spiritual community for belonging. When and where you gather is up to you. The point is to gather. To become vulnerable again. To open up and share and listen and trust that healthy and life-giving relationships are possible again among God's people. We can and should *be the church* for the sake of one another and to provide hope to a fallen world. We cannot do this in isolation. This does not happen in exile.

I believe what I've written here with all my heart. I also wrestle to open myself up again; to become vulnerable, to trust others and hope they won't kick me when I'm down as they have a few times before. I've seen behind some curtains, and I've outgrown my youthful naivete. Some churches are unhealthy. Some church leaders are corrupt. Sometimes church people can be bigger stinkers than your pagan neighbors. These things are all true. Some of you know all too well. But we need each other. To the exiles who have read all the way to the end: know that you matter. Know that our churches need you. I need you. You have a story to tell and talents to use. You bear the image of God, and we need desperately to see it. I'm trying to reengage the best I can, myself. I'm slowly and carefully testing the waters as I attempt my own journey from exile back into Christian community. I stand with you in fear and reluctance. I'm not excited to deal with any stinkers on the horizon, and I'm very aware that I am often a stinker myself. You probably stink sometimes too. I will try not to be a stinker if you agree to not be a stinker in return. This may be what it all boils down to when living in Christian community.

To those in exile: know that you matter, you are loved, and you are needed. We need to hear your stories and learn from your experiences. You bear the image of God, and we need to see it. You have been created with a divine purpose and gifted uniquely for kingdom service. Someone somewhere owes you an apology that you will probably never receive. I get it. This is my story too. I stand with you. Even more, I would love to stand with you—literally. We don't have to talk, necessarily; we won't hold hands or make it weird. We can simply be. In our hurt. In our disillusionment. In our hope that God's people have more to offer than what we have sometimes experienced in the past. May we move together from exile into community. Slowly. Carefully. Faithfully.

DISCUSSION 5

Text—1 Corinthians 12:12–26; Ephesians 4:1–16

1. Have you ever been hurt or excluded by God's people? Do you know someone else who has been negatively affected through similar experiences? If you are comfortable, please share a little about these experiences.

2. What do people mean when they claim to be "spiritual but not religious"? Is it possible to be a Christian without any need for community with God's people?

3. Ephesians 4:1–16 speaks to the unity God desires for his people. What attitudes and actions are mentioned specifically to achieve and maintain unity in the local church? Describe the community envisioned here. What roles do you and I play in this congregation?

4. What has been your experience with unity among God's people? To what extent do we preach, practice, and prioritize this concept in our churches?

5. In 1 Cor 12:12–26, Paul speaks of the church as a (unified) body with many parts. What is the natural outcome for churches who estrange and exile people who might otherwise be active in their midst? Conversely, can exiled believers utilize spiritual gifts to their fullest extent without need of a church with which to participate? Explain.

6. Where do we even begin to nurture healthier churches that enliven the principles found in the passages above? How do we convince exiles we are serious about all this? If you are an exile, what would it take to convince you any church is seriously committed to these principles?

7. Imagine a church in which people put others' needs ahead of their own. Imagine if people in this church committed to attitudes of mutual submission and lifestyles of humble servitude. Could such a church exist today? Will such a church ever exist on this side of heaven?

6. Stages

HERE'S WHERE I LOSE some readers in my Church of Christ circles. How do I know? Because I've been raised in, educated by, and employed on behalf of Churches of Christ for as long as I can remember. I know my people, and I know many of them won't like what follows. This next little bit is not solely a commentary on my tribe. What follows is for anyone who has experienced the North American variety of venue-based evangelicalism, regardless of denominational titles or institutional brands. I *start* with my tribe, as these are the people I know best. Go ahead and "write me up" in Alabama and Tennessee. Ban me from your lectures if you haven't already. I often wonder if being "disfellowshipped" in certain circles is affirmation for good and healthy ministry. Another chapter for a different occasion.

Two disclaimers before stating my case—read these and take them seriously. First, theology is important—for you, for me, and for our churches. What we believe about God, his people, and his will for creation. I assume you agree, or you wouldn't waste time reading this publication. *All that we do as God's people should be rooted in theological reflection and application.* This principle applies to Sunday morning worship assemblies and to my interactions with others in secular contexts throughout the week. We must always think about who we are and what we do in relation to our understanding of God and his purposes. Theology matters. Most of us could afford to think more theologically about even the mundane things of life.

Second, doctrine is essential. Again—for you and me, as parents, friends, coworkers, and personal evangelists. Doctrine is *especially* essential for our churches. Things we discern from Scripture that provide guidance for how to live as God's people. How to resolve conflicts. How to honor our spouses. How to worship, how to make disciples, how to evangelize our neighborhoods, how to be good taxpayers and responsible citizens—the application of scriptural precedent to our personal and communal expressions of *life* as worship. Doctrine is rooted in theology; the resulting, systematic expression of practices we espouse and embrace as congruent with our understanding of Scripture. Theology is what we believe; doctrine is what we teach because of what we believe. Churches hold to a variety of doctrines, whether explicitly stated or not. Some doctrines are taught, others are caught. (Another promising topic for a future occasion.)

Here is the reality we often fail to recognize. While it seems like doctrine should *proceed from* theology, the truth is that doctrine and theology are mutually informative, each shaping the other. In some cases, our doctrines (what we teach and prescribe as acceptable practice) have shaped our theology (what we believe about God, his people, and his will for creation). My tribe has done this with issues of worship (the Bible does not prescribe a cappella worship any more than it condemns instrumentation) and lifestyle (the Bible does not condemn moderate and responsible consumption of alcohol). In each of these cases, historically and contextually based practices (lack of available instruments after the Civil War; demonization of alcohol through Prohibition) have resulted in teachings (doctrines) that have affected our theology. We don't use instruments in worship, and we don't consume alcohol because "these things are wrong in God's eyes and possible grounds for eternal damnation." In these cases, doctrine has become primary, informing our theology. Had we started with *theology*, our conclusions, our teachings, and our resulting practices may have been different.

When theology informs our doctrines, we encounter new challenges. If our belief is in a gracious and benevolent God (as it should be), we can sometimes embrace practices that are incongruent with scriptural precedent, simply because we can't imagine a good and gracious God to prescribe or enforce any standard of practice construed is discriminatory through our subjective, culturally conditioned interpretive framework. When it comes to matters of gender, this is a huge issue for our churches. Not a new issue by any means, simply one that has become more pressing with the evolution of our cultural norms. Did God really intend women to be silent in our assemblies? We love to fight over this issue. Proponents of gender inclusion cite Gal 3; opponents ground themselves in 1 Cor 11. We can (and do) argue this issue either way, each perspective resulting from underlying theological convictions about God—his will, his character, his intentions for all of creation as presented in Scripture. Every church must prayerfully study and form conclusions about God's will in these matters. Not every church will agree, and we must accept variance of resulting doctrines here. Sorry, that's just how it is.

There's a third piece to this equation. This is this part I wish to address. The ultimate expression of theology (what we believe) and doctrine (what we teach) is played out both in our individual lives and through corporate expression by our *practices* (what we do and how we do, resulting from our actual convictions). Practices say more about our theology and doctrine than any creedal statement or curricular presentation. On a personal level, this is a sobering reality. The lived-out reality of your faith is found in who you are and how you act toward others. For better and worse, you and I *live* what we believe. Collectively, for our churches, the unfortunate reality is how often we elevate practice over theology and doctrine, justifying means, modes, and methods of being and "doing" church without critical evaluation. Corporate practices do as much to shape a people as any theological supposition or doctrinal statement ever will. What we do when we gather says much about what we value and why we gather at all. My concern is that for many churches, practice has so overshadowed theology and doctrine that we have created an expression of "church" that is incongruent with examples found on our New Testament. Preferential practices (what we like, how we like it, how these things make us feel, and how marketable these things may be) outweigh theology and doctrine in this threefold equation. Practices have evolved in our corporate gatherings so that stages have become our centerpieces, sometimes more than Jesus himself. Things said and done from stages receive more time, attention, scrutiny, and dollars than anything else that occurs within and among our churches. We gather to worship Jesus—this is what we claim. We often worship *stages*. This is our practice.

Suffice it to say, I'm not a fan of stages. I appreciate them at concert venues, I just don't love them in our church buildings. My church has one, yours likely does too. The Bible doesn't prescribe or condemn these, they are simply products of corporate practice in which some of our people are elevated to be audible and visible to others. The bigger the crowd, the more necessary these become. Stages serve a practical purpose in this regard, and I don't think there is anything inherently wrong with having one or two or three in our corporate meeting spaces (yes, I've been to churches who have multiple of these in various rooms and auditoriums). I'm simply not a fan. Here's why.

Have you ever considered how much of your church's budget is directed toward things that occur on or around stages? The amount here is significant. The people we employ for ministry are evaluated and enumerated based largely on what they do on stages. This is true for pulpit preachers and senior pastors, as well as any who are paid to lead worship in our corporate assemblies. To varying degrees, these same criteria are applied to ministers of all kinds. Paid ministers speak and teach as part of their jobs—things often done from stages. Beyond investments in paid staff, consider the financial resources given to outfitting our stages with technology and aesthetic treatments that make them functional and appealing. How much does it cost to remodel a stage (or auditorium, or youth room, or foyer area) every now and then to keep it from looking outdated? Has your church transitioned from analog to digital for all your AV needs? Some of these improvements cost more than you realize. All these things are necessary for churches with stages. Why elevate anyone to a stage if we can't see or hear or stream or project them in a way that is functional and appealing? I wonder if Jesus suffered for lack of stage in his sermons on the mount and plains. Church budgets and stage presentations are interrelated to disproportionate amounts when we honestly assess our allocation of resources.

More than financial liabilities, stages are often the cause for fighting and division among our people. Churches in my tribe fight more about worship styles and gender roles in our worship assemblies than any other topic on the planet. Our churches split over these issues. Long-held friendships and biological families are torn apart through different opinions on these matters. I've seen this my whole life. Worship styles and gender roles, worship styles and gender roles. Ugh. What does this all boil down to? *Who is allowed on our stages, and what are they allowed to do there?* Where? *On the stage.* At the center of our corporate assembly. At the epicenter of our Christian experience (so it seems).

Maybe your denomination functions differently. In my tribe, we *think* our conflicts and divisions are largely related to worship styles and gender roles. Unfortunately, we are misguided in our thinking. Our issues are *not* primarily about worship or gender— our issues are related to the elevation (pun intended) of stages as our central focal point for corporate assemblies, the primary location (so we think) for our deepest and most important spiritual experiences. We sit and stand and kneel; we lift hands and give amens—all in the direction of our stages and the people who speak and sing and perform from them. Think about the configuration of the worship spaces in your church. Chances are, yours is set up this way too. While born of practical need, the resulting practice has confused our thinking and shifted our focus. The stage has become our centerpiece. What happens there is most important of all—especially on Sundays because those few hours on Sunday morning are the ones most of us believe matter most of all. *We fight over worship and gender because these issues have been elevated with the stages on which they occur.* People talk and debate and fight and divide over matters they hold dear. As far as I can tell, the things that happen *on the stages of our churches* must be the most important things in all the universe—we hold these *most* dearly. While these should be matters of theology and doctrine, the reality here is an argument based in practices, at venues, under spotlights, *on stages*.

I attended a Sunday evening home group a few months ago. At this meeting, people worshiped, read from Scripture, shared and reflected together in guided conversation, and at the very end, took the Lord's Supper. The person who "passed our trays" that night was a little girl, probably in the third or fourth grade. Nobody took issue with this. Was she a believer? Had she been baptized? Was she in a place of greater authority than me or the guy sitting next to me because she was actively serving while we passively received? This was a beautiful experience that would not be allowed in most Sunday morning assemblies. Why? Not because of age or gender or baptism or "authority" of any real kind—this would be seen as inappropriate *from a stage*. This little girl was free to bring Communion elements from kitchen to living room. Carrying the same elements from stage to pew is somehow viewed differently.

There is something formal we assign to stages in church auditoriums. People on stages hold "authority" that others do not. Imagine everything you do on a typical Sunday morning in your church. What would be right and acceptable in this environment? What would our explicit and implicit doctrines intend for this time and space. Now imagine all these things—the very same acts of worship—played out in your living room. Things change when we remove our stages. Things change when we sit together in different environments and configurations. What happens when we sit in a circle? Side by side and visible to one another, not looking past the back of others' heads, craning to see and hear from people on a stage? What if our speakers and worship leaders sit next to us in that circle? What if our host at the home group our house church provides a meal (you likely assume that host to be female), and offers to also serve our communion? You would think of this differently. Why? None of these examples are in auditoriums with stages and lights and microphones and "authority" assigned to those who stand on elevated platforms.

When it comes to gender roles in our worship assemblies, remove the stage and remove the issue. Similar may be said of our comfort levels with various styles of worship. Different places and different spaces—without use of stages and platforms and all the bells and whistles (sometimes literally)—lead to different experiences and different thinking on these matters. Yes, there are additional layers to discern here for my tribe (and yours). Theology and doctrine are important. In these cases, our doctrine and practice have become convoluted to affect our theological convictions, often without critical reflection or even a willingness to consider the congruency of our practices and beliefs. We determine this and that are "right" or "wrong" based on what we have always seen and done in our immediate circles. Theology is born of practice. Doctrines related to these themes are taught and caught, often implicitly. We really have some work to do here.

For now, please consider my argument. *Our fights and divisions over gender roles are often really fights over stages.* To some extent, the same is true for arguments over worship styles and formats, the need for worship orders and finely tuned worship sets. (Yes, a cappella song leaders have their own versions of these. You will see this if you pay attention. It's all there to see, every Sunday morning, on a stage at the front of your auditorium.) Remove the stage and remove these issues. Or, if you prefer, remove the stage *and at the very least* reframe these conversations. Think about it.

Lastly, whether we intend this or not, stages perpetuate an often shallow and consumeristic experience of Christianity based more on *venue* than virtue. Venue-based spirituality is killing our churches. We love to gather crowds, to count heads and count dollars and expand our facilities for bigger stages on which even better and more talented speakers and worship leaders and performers can offer their services. We create venues for people to gather and share experiences for an hour or two every Sunday. These spaces are expensive to build and maintain, and much is expected of the paid professionals who operate on the stages within. We assume that better facilities with nicer amenities will attract more people, younger people, maybe families with teenagers and children. We know they won't sit through boring sermons, and we certainly owe them a dynamic worship experience. Why? To keep them coming back. To what? To our venue-based experience of the Christ life in which all that ever happens or really matters is that which occurs on stages in auditoriums as facilitated by paid professionals whose employment is based on how well they perform on these very same stages.

We know this intuitively, don't we? If stage lights or fog machines or louder guitars or shaped notes on your overhead projector add to an overall pleasant and enjoyable experience, you will certainly appeal to a portion of our consumer evangelical market. There will always be consumer Christians among us. Not everyone will pick up their cross. I'm not sure we are helping by advancing a paradigm for "church" that *occurs on stages* in auditoriums on Sunday mornings. Our churches need to stop making their weekly worship assemblies the most overplanned, overfunded, overstaffed, overcommunicated, overdone, overargued about, overdivided, overemphasized, central purpose and offering for our people and for the fallen world who needs so much *more* than presentations from stages on Sunday mornings.

Ours has become a venue-based form of religion—a venue-based experience of the Christian life in its "fullest" expression. This does little for the people beyond our walls. If we aren't careful, this also keeps the people within our walls shallow, immature, and wanting more from our venues when the preaching gets old, or the worship becomes stale, or there aren't enough programs for all our kids concurrent with the gathered assembly of paying adults. The point is to live *beyond* these walls. The time has come to decentralize our venue-based thinking, our venue-based offerings. I've heard it said: "What we win people with is what we win people to." *Many of our churches, even with good intentions, are winning people to presentations and programs that occur on stages at venues, and nothing more.* Stages communicate much about our theology, doctrine, and practice. Not just what we say and do from these platforms, but the centrality of these platforms to the life and experience of our churches, in general. Our stages say more than we realize. Maybe it's time we think twice about what we are saying to our people and what we are communicating (or not) to a world in need of Jesus.

DISCUSSION 6

Text—1 Corinthians 14:26–40; Ephesians 5:19–20

1. What is your initial reaction to this chapter? Does the writer make a valid point or is this simply an overreaction to contemporary practices in our churches?

2. Identify some industries and careers that rely heavily on stages. Who are the people on these stages? What is their job? How are they evaluated and by whom? Is there anything cautionary here for churches and their leaders whose primary ministries occur on stages?

3. First Corinthians 14:26–40 is uncomfortable for some. Read these verses and compare the practices mentioned here to those employed in the corporate worship assemblies of your own congregation. Are there any issues you see here that require further study? Explain.

4. Ephesians 5:19–20 speaks of musical expressions of worship among God's people. Modes of musical expression are open to interpretation here. What role do stages play in the facilitation of musical worship in Christian assemblies? Outline the pros and cons related to this issue.

5. Do you agree that practices associated with corporate worship assemblies are interpreted and evaluated differently when stages become involved? Explain.

6. What can we do to ensure people on stages don't become stars of a show or centerpieces of a commercial offering? How do we keep stages from becoming exclusive?

7. Imagine a church without a stage. Imagine a people who gather to worship God and encourage one another, with some who teach and some who pray and some who serve Communion. Imagine a church where prophets share in turn and tongues are not forbidden. Imagine a church where age and race and gender are all things to be valued as necessary parts of a larger whole in which Jesus is shown and shared with the community beyond our doors. What would this church look like—with or without a stage?

7. Gifts

I TOOK A SPIRITUAL gift assessment recently. This was not my first, not even my second or third. I have checked the boxes on a variety of these over the years. As a lifelong student of social sciences, I've always been intrigued with these instruments. Despite the "spiritual" intent of these resources, I recognize all as imperfect, human means of assessing qualities that may reflect as much about your personality, temperament, and birth order as they do about your God-infused talents and Spirit-enabled purposes for kingdom service. Nevertheless, I still enjoy a well-crafted instrument that provides better assessment of my *self*, my strengths, and my potentials.

Some of you are on board with me here. Maybe you're a fan of the MBTI (Myers-Briggs Type Indicator), or you've appreciated the insights of a DISC (Dominance, Inducement, Steadiness, Compliance) inventory. Maybe you prefer the Clifton Strengths Finder. Some of you know already if you are a golden retriever or an otter, and others have proudly discovered which Harry Potter and Star Wars characters hold the most similar personalities to their own. Then there are the Enneagram people. We often experience these as Enneagram evangelists. As one of the least scientific theories available, in recent years, this resource has gained one of the most passionate followings.

Others of you rolled your eyes two paragraphs ago. I'm not sure why you've read this far, but I'm thankful you're following. To this group, human inventories are mostly a waste of time. Even our first group must admit that pop culture assessments designed to tell you which character you would be in a Disney movie are basically stupid. Maybe there's a place for vocational assessments among guidance counselors and educators to assist young people in charting a course beyond high school. Maybe the Clifton Strengths Finder can provide helpful insights about job candidates we consider as future hires. Beyond these, most assessments hold value as tools for personal entertainment.

We can be friends regardless of how you feel about all this. Human instruments will forever be flawed. Despite their limitations, I often discover fascinating insights about myself and others when I give these a chance. I am a textbook firstborn according to birth order theory. I align fairly well with other ISTJs. Supposedly, I have strengths in learning, input, and intellection. I couldn't tell you which Avenger I would be because I really don't care. And for those who are wondering, I am very much a One Wing Two on the Enneagram. There you go.

In the language of spiritual gifts, I always register strongly in three areas. I am an administrator, a teacher, and a prophet. Administration is typically my primary gifting among the three. In this case, the assessments I've taken appear spot on. I know what you're thinking. "Administration? Hooray! Who doesn't love a good administrator? You must be the life of the party everywhere you go!" Settle down, friends. This gift is not always as glamorous as you might expect.

Stereotypically, youth ministers are not known for their administrative gifts. My colleagues are typically seen as poor managers of time, budgets, and communications. Youth workers are *stereotypically* disorganized and impulsive, more like flighty teenagers, less like responsible adults. Sadly, we have earned this reputation for ourselves. Youth workers often exhibit these traits, the hiring practices of many churches only exacerbating these issues. Churches hire fun people as their youth workers. Fun people are not always mature, responsible, or even *thinking* people. Fun people are not always organized. Unfortunately, churches don't evaluate these qualities at the point of hire. In my experience, the administrative qualities necessary to lead groups of people—especially in youth ministry—are undervalued until the respective leader(s) overspend, under communicate, or prove unreliable. Youth workers are hired for big personalities and infectious enthusiasm; they are often fired for shortcomings in administration. I've been fired, myself. Never for this reason.

For my Enneagram people out there, here's my theory. Churches want Threes in their pulpits and Sevens in their youth ministry departments. In other words, we want "performers" on our stages and "enthusiasts" leading our youth groups. As an Enneagram One (the "reformer"), I don't fit neatly into either of these categories. I question performers who can sometimes be inauthentic. I envy the enthusiasts (the *actual* life of the party people) as one geared for practicality. I don't encounter many churches looking for administrators in their youth ministry departments. I rarely find administrators in our pulpits.

Here's the rub for someone like me. The administration thing is both a blessing and a curse. Positively, I am an organized and responsible person. I can see the big picture, break things down into functional components, analyze and assess, create structures, systems, and practices to help myself and others be more effective and efficient. I can track all this on a spreadsheet, present it from the front of the room, develop the training program, and create the curriculum to advance our initiatives. I don't mind the research, and I am excited to share insights with others—especially those with potential to make us more effective in fulfilling our purpose and more efficient in achieving our goals. This is my wheelhouse. I *think* God wired me this way. I think?

Vocationally, this gift has been a liability in the field of professional ministry. My background is largely in ministry with teenagers and families. In this world, people care less about big picture and more about activity. Youth ministry, as often conceived and practiced, is more about how to have fun, how to keep our venues packed, how to bait people and keep them coming back for more, than it ever is about *why* we do these things, or *what we are accomplishing* through our approaches and related programming. I've never been comfortable with this. It is well documented that significant numbers of youth group kids drop out of church after high school. We've known this for years. We lament this in our churches as students vanish over time. Yet, our approaches to youth ministry remain largely unchanged. Why would we expect different results when we keep doing the same things, year after year, decade after decade? Churches are guilty of short-term thinking here. We don't assess or evaluate with an end in mind. We fail to ask *why* we do this or that and *what* we hope to achieve beyond a full house at the next hyped event. I've pushed back against all this (my prophetic gift). I've asked lots of questions. I've refused to embrace the status quo. I've created and presented alternative approaches to student ministry in various settings (my teaching gift). Some churches, some parent groups, and some search committees have appreciated these more than others. At the end of the day, most churches just want youth workers who are fun for the kids and at least moderately capable of relating to their parents. Administrators need not apply.

In my experience, preachers and senior pastors are also cut from a different cloth. I rarely find administrators in their ranks either. Administrative types who serve as underlings in the staffing hierarchy (aka youth pastors) encounter vocational hazards here. I've worked with some incredible people who were self-secure and humble enough to empower me to use my gifts without things getting weird. I have thrived once or twice in my career when the person in *power* appreciated my potential and allowed me to operate from my strengths. More commonly, I have encountered frustration and conflict. When people in power are insecure—these are most of the people you know in professional ministry—they typically don't appreciate underlings who ask questions about efficiencies and effectiveness. Administrative types can't help seeing and thinking about such things. Our challenge is to know when to speak up and when to keep our mouths shut when we identify things that could function differently to achieve favorable outcomes. Insecure leaders wrestling with pride, ego, and job security; those who seek the spotlights; and those who live for the strokes of others rarely appreciate the value of underling administrators on their teams. Administrators are liabilities here. Threats, real or perceived.

The most commonly cited treatments of spiritual gifts in the New Testament are found in Rom 12, 1 Cor 12, Eph 4, and 1 Pet 4. I encourage you to read these for yourself if you haven't already. Read the entirety of these chapters; read the ones before and after. Consider the context of these writings and how these passages relate to the whole of the books in which they are found. This is how we should always approach the text. Pause here and read these now if you like.

Some of you already know how God has gifted you. Maybe you've also played around with the inventories and assessments. Maybe you have just lived long enough to know your own strengths and weaknesses. Hopefully, you have been affirmed of your gift(s) from others who recognize and appreciate your potential. I suspect many from this group can identify and align with the words, concepts, and roles outlined in the four texts above. Some of us are encouragers, others full of mercy, still others gifted as apostles (small "a"—those who are sent out to share their faith with new people in new places). If you've identified your gift and it has been affirmed by others, praise God! I am convinced this is part of the discipleship process. *Every follower of Jesus needs to gain some understanding of how they are wired, and for what purpose, so they can live intentionally to bless others and honor God in their own unique way.* Certainly, God's design for the church is that of a mutually-supportive community in which a diversity of gifts is implemented for the strengthening of the whole—to the glory of God, and for the hope of a fallen world. In the church, every person is gifted in some form or fashion to support and build up others. Whatever your gift, the church needs you to identify and use it.

This leads us to the rest who have read this far. Those without a clue what their gifts may be, how they would know, and what to do with them once discovered. If this describes you, that's totally okay. I was raised in churches that didn't talk much about all this. I've *worked* with churches that didn't talk much about all this. If you took the time to read the texts above, you're already off to a good start in your journey of gift discovery. Certainly, these passages don't contain a definitive listing of every talent or ability you may have to serve God and others. Maybe you are good with technology. Maybe your thing is music, or poetry, or painting, or humor, or cooking. Our understanding of spiritual gifts begins in the text (those things we find specifically mentioned) and expands to include other talents and abilities we have at our disposal for the glory of God. I am open-minded enough to assume the ways God equips his people, and the purposes he has for their equipping, goes beyond the text here. Even if you haven't nailed down your gift(s) yet, I suspect you have a hunch about your own strengths and weaknesses. Maybe a spiritual gift inventory will be helpful to you as well. Certainly, a conversation with someone who knows you well and will tell you the truth about what they see in you is a tremendous opportunity for personal growth and self-understanding. I encourage you to explore all of these. Prayerfully. Ask God to reveal your gift(s) so you may recognize, embrace, and further develop these to his glory. The church needs you. We need you to be you to your fullest and for you to do your thing.

I wrestle with how to use my gifts these days. The administrator in me seeks opportunities to administrate something. If God really *did* wire me this way, I trust he will provide something that enables me to serve from my strength—eventually. As for the prophecy piece, I suppose what you are reading stems from this gift in some way or another. I write when I feel like there is something that needs to be said. My teaching gift is one I find uses for regularly. I am currently teaching my third teenager to drive. So far, so good. What I don't currently understand is how all these things are supposed to work together for the purpose of *ministry* at this point in time, during this season, this next chapter of my life. For years I enjoyed work that required each of these gifts to be exercised in ways that nurtured and advanced the kingdom. People didn't often appreciate my administrative bent, nor did they always like my prophetic voice. The teaching part was expected, and I always did well with this. I think I did *fairly* well with my work in general. I *think*? (At least two churches and their senior pastors would disagree.) Over the years, I took for granted the opportunities to use my particular gifts in professional ministry on a daily basis—while *getting paid* for this! I did things I enjoyed that I considered meaningful and important. I engaged tasks for which I was well suited (in most cases). The work of professional (paid) ministry enabled, even *required* me to use those things God instilled within me as I fulfilled a (somewhat) defined role in his kingdom. Now, my work is different. I have the same gifts to offer, but without the institution, the office, the budget, the people and programs, the classroom or curriculum. Administrators need something to administrate. I think.

What about you? Where are you in the process of discovery and development when it comes to your own giftedness? Every person has something to offer in service to God and his kingdom. You have something you were wired to do in this life. Can you identify and describe your gift(s) to others? Have you found outlets and opportunities to develop your gift(s) as you seek to honor God *for creating you this way in the first place*? If the answer is no, you have work to do. Experiment with an inventory. Ask a friend what gift(s) they see in you. Pray for God to make these clear—*and* for opportunities to use your gift(s) in ways that deepen, broaden, and advance his kingdom. I pray for this myself. I pray that God leads me to wherever I am supposed to be, to do whatever I am supposed to do for him. I must believe somewhere along the way God will present opportunities that require the gifts he has given me. I believe this for you as well. If only we look and listen and stand ready to be obedient. May we both recognize these opportunities and act faithfully to do whatever those things are that God places in front of us. May we use our gifts for his glory.

DISCUSSION 7

Text—Romans 12:1–8; 1 Corinthians 12:1–11;
Ephesians 4:11–16; 1 Peter 4:7–11

1. Describe your own experience with instruments that measure traits in personality, temperament, or spiritual giftedness. What have you learned from your own assessments? What is your opinion of these instruments?

2. What are your spiritual gifts? Why do you assume this? Is there any way to know for sure?

3. Read and compare the above texts from Romans and 1 Corinthians. List the gifts that are mentioned collectively in these passages. Which of these do you encounter most commonly in other Christians? Which appear less common? How do we account for this? Explain.

4. Identify some people you know who clearly exhibit one or more of the gifts found in these passages. How do these people use their gifts to serve God and others? Did you mention people other than professional ministers and pastors? To what extent does our thinking about spiritual gifts begin and end with those in various forms of paid ministry?

5. Describe your experience with churches and their appreciation for spiritual gifts among their members. To what extent have these churches discovered, developed, and deployed the gifts of their people for intentional service to God and others?

6. What do the passages in Eph 4 and 1 Pet 4 contribute to our understanding about the nature and purpose of spiritual gifts among God's people? What imperatives do these verses hold for you and me as children of God, uniquely gifted for his purposes?

7. Imagine a church in which every person discovered, developed, and deployed their gifts for service to God and others. Imagine if every person here was valued and appreciated for having something unique to contribute and share. What would this church look like? How would it function? What challenges and opportunities exist here?

8. Pills

You ARE GIVEN THE choice of two pills. Take the blue pill and everything you *think* you know remains unchanged. Take the red pill and discover the realities of life—the things that are, and have been, and will continue to be, that you have never *actually* known at all. The blue pill is nothing really, a placebo to some and a sedative for others. Blue pills allow us to live in blissful naivete. The red pill is different. Red pills open eyes to realities that are often disappointing, sometimes painful, and occasionally horrific.

Fans of *The Matrix* recognize this scenario as the basic premise of a series of movies that suggests an underlying reality of which we are all unaware. In these films, Neo takes the red pill and discovers the entirety of his perceived existence has been a lie. The red pill reveals to Neo that his perceived reality is an illusion. In *reality*, Neo is merely an electrical component in the Matrix—a giant computer system that programs people to experience a projected world they believe is real, while their actual bodies serve as power supplies in an elaborate network of circuitry behind the scenes. When Neo takes the red pill, he awakens; his eyes are opened. Reality is exposed. The world gets turned on its head. Make sense? Better to just watch the movie. The first one is excellent.

I've taken some red pills. The older I get, the more I can recall. Unlike Neo in *The Matrix*, I haven't always had a choice of red or blue. Sometimes life feeds us red pills whether we want them or not. Sometimes we experience realities that open our eyes to things we never would have believed; things we never, ever wanted to know. Red pills change the way we see the world, they strip us of our innocence and obliterate naïveté. The red pill is a hard pill to swallow.

As a kid, I was a huge Star Wars fan. I loved the lightsabers and laser blasters and spaceships. I loved the weird creatures and different planets. Star Wars was all about fantasy and adventure and star pilots blowing up space stations. As a kid, this was basically all I saw, all I understood, all I cared to know about the plot or storyline in general. Star Wars was the best movie ever, the entire premise summed up in the title. The end.

Somewhere in my teenage years it hit me. One day, as I sat down for my millionth viewing of Star Wars (VHS edition in our family VCR), I suddenly put the pieces together. Star Wars was never about the things I had loved as a child. Yes, the action and adventure were always there. But under all that, from start to finish, and throughout about six thousand sequels and spin-offs, Star Wars had always been and continues to be about two things: religion and politics. It took more than one Mountain Dew to wash that red pill down. Religion and politics, the most taboo of all subjects among sensible adults who don't enjoy family arguments at Thanksgiving dinner or awkward conversations in their workplaces. My favorite movie was just a fanciful drama about religion and politics . . .

This was a red pill awakening for me. I would never experience Star Wars quite the same way again. Surely you experienced something like this as you moved through childhood and into adolescence. We all found out about Santa Claus, the Easter Bunny, and the Tooth Fairy at some point, didn't we? All of these were red pill awakenings. Few of us asked to take these red pills. One day they just fell into our Kool-Aid. Maybe somewhere in elementary school you learned that Kermit was just a puppet who lived in a shoebox between tapings. Maybe you watched the space shuttle explode on live television and realized that real life starships were nothing like the ones in your favorite movies. If only *that* crew could have returned for an award ceremony. Red pills can be *very* hard to swallow.

Teenage years come with many red pills. I assume this is true for every generation. We Gen Xers had our own version of this. Maybe you thought the presidency was reserved for morally upright and respectable people. Enter Bill Clinton. Here's your pill. Maybe you wore flannels and jeans and Timberland boots and secretly wanted to move to Seattle. That is, until Kurt Cobain committed suicide and you watched the reports every time you turned on MTV or VH1. You mean to tell me presidents can be adulterers and rock stars can be unhappy, depressed, and lonely? Red pills all around. I could say more here about the Gulf War, the Oklahoma City bombing, and the Columbine shooting. These were giant red pill awakenings for my generation, intense experiences of reality that woke us up to pain and fear and loss and distrust and anxiety and insecurity like we had never known before. All this, with 9/11 just over the horizon. Red pills wake us to realities that are hard to believe and sometimes painful to accept. Pills like these choke us on their way down. There's not enough water in the world to get them down without a struggle.

Maybe this is why, as an adult, I sometimes choose the blue pills in life. I have so enjoyed our family trips to Disney World, that I never want to know what goes on behind the scenes there. You know what I'm talking about. That place is magical to me and the memories I have there are precious. Give me the blue pill and let me believe that place is perfect! You might feel this way about your favorite restaurant. Imagine if you knew how dirty that kitchen might be or how long they use food past the expiration dates. Blue pills allow us to imagine things as we want them to be. Red pills sometimes reveal that people are spitting in the milkshakes at our favorite ice cream shop. Blue pills are bliss. Kinda.

Here's the thing. Wouldn't you *want* to know if someone was spitting in all your milkshakes? Take the blue pill and keep sucking down others' loogies or take the red pill and immediately stop going to that ice cream shop. This seems like a no-brainer to me. But what if those milkshakes are from my favorite ice cream shop *at Disney World*? Arrrgh! Now I have a dilemma. Blue pill or red pill? Why can't people just keep their loogies to themselves? We can't escape the red pills of life, and I'm not sure it's a good idea to live with our heads in the sand. Sometimes we need to swallow a red pill so we can grow and mature. Sometimes red pills are the *best* medicine. This doesn't make them any easier to swallow.

Professional ministry has been a series of red pill awakenings for me over the years. I remember the first time I saw the unused communion elements splattered all over the trash can where they were discarded earlier that week. I had never considered what happened to the juice and crackers that weren't consumed on Sunday. That image is still burned into my brain. The body and the blood—in a white plastic trash can outside the church office. Red pill. I remember the first time I watched a preacher stomp out of an elders meeting. I never knew things like this happened. Red pill. I've taken red pills every time I learned of a minister who cheated on their spouse or ran away with a work associate. Some with *teenagers*. Big nasty red pill. I remember the first person I knew personally who decided to destroy his life and others around him. I am praying for another friend who made this same choice recently. I've taken too many of those red pills over the years. As for churches in general? I've seen parents behave like children and elders act like dictators. I've been victimized by politics and abused by power. Red pills. I've seen people with money control churches and their leaders. I've watched family clans do the same thing. Red pills. I've worked with paid church staff who should have been fired, and I've known a few who were dismissed unfairly. I've accepted that Star Wars and church work have the same things in common: *religion and politics*. I took that red pill years ago.

Youth ministry has been my wheelhouse all these years. I think most of us who pursue this line of work do so with a Nerf gun in one hand and a pile of blue pills in the other. We know that teenagers are awesome, and we love the idea of ministry outside of pulpits and classrooms. We pop the blue pills as long as we can. If we do this work long enough, we encounter teen runaways, pregnancies, and suicide attempts. Eventually, we report someone to the authorities for physical or sexual abuse. Usually we report an adult, sometimes we report a teenager. I've had to do both. All these are big, fat, nasty red pill experiences for any youth worker worth their salt. I have a youth worker friend whose students were in Columbine High School the day of that horrific shooting. He sat with victims and ministered to survivors. How's that for a boulder-sized red pill? I have another youth worker friend whose van wrecked on a youth group trip. There were casualties. There were questions that could not be answered. Big, jagged, nasty red pill. Both these men know loss. Both have seen horrors. Both know the deep pain of red pill experiences on the darkest days of ministry with young people. I wonder how many people enter the ranks of professional ministry without a clue; blissfully naive and blind to what awaits. I suspect most. Praise God for anyone in ministry who can swallow pills like these and still find the strength to get up the next morning and engage their craft again.

I've taken enough red pills to have a different view of the church these days. I used to believe the church was a safe place. Sadly, this is not always true. I used to think church people could be trusted. Again, this has not always been my experience. As a kid, I just assumed churches were full of awesome people who loved Jesus and loved each other, and all got along and wanted to be together as often as possible. Then one day, as a teenager, I learned of a deacon who went to jail for embezzling money out of the collection plates. What? In my twenties, I worked with a church leadership in which the preacher and elders communicated by written correspondence for a season because they couldn't work together in the same room. Are you kidding me? By my thirties, I had called Child Protective Services a few times. This was becoming routine. I wasn't prepared for the deaths, divorces, and family dysfunction that I also encountered during these years. Ugh. Red pills. So far, my forties have been worst of all. At least, on a personal level. I've seen the worst of people in power who control their churches from behind the scenes. I've been disillusioned by some slick elders, some insecure ministers, and a pastor's wife who reminded me that *power* does not reside in titles, paychecks, or job descriptions when it comes to the inner workings of the church. I've seen behind enough curtains to know there is always something happening behind the scenes that is less than awesome. I've taken too many red pills to believe differently at this point. Some churches are healthier than others, and some of our leaders are pure hearted enough to be confused by my comments above. There are plenty of good and righteous people out there doing good and right things inside and out of our churches. These are *most* of the people I've known in my service to the church. If only *all* our people behaved this way.

I feel a responsibility to share all this with you and others. Not to sour you on the church. Not to make you suspicious or distrusting. I hope we can all find a healthy balance of blue and red pills when it comes to our experience and understanding of our respective churches. For me, this means stepping back from a formal leadership role with my current congregation. At least for a season. I don't want to serve on any committees or task forces right now. I don't want to see behind this curtain. I don't want to take the red pills that inevitably come with more formal engagement. I just need a blue pill season for now. Let me be ignorant for a while. Let me pretend that everything is fine and dandy. Clearly, there's a danger in this. Too many blue pills, over too long a stretch, can be unhealthy. Blue pill people can be naive to a fault. Immature. Blind. Careless. Drinkers of others' loogies at the ice cream parlor, simply because they are unwilling to engage with reality. We have plenty of this in our churches already. If we took a red pill every now and then, maybe we could have some different conversations about who we are and what we do and why any of this matters at all. Red pills illuminate our thinking and create possibilities for accountability. Red pills force us to deal with reality, whether we like it or not. Quit calling yourself a "one-thousand-member church" when you consistently gather three hundred. Take a red pill and embrace your reality. Quit planning events for your own kids in the name of "community outreach." Those bouncy houses are great, but let's be honest about who they are *actually* for in the first place. Take your red pill already. And if the mantra at your church is "service" and you consistently struggle to find volunteers for your ministry programs? This seems like a red pill opportunity to me.

Some of you have walked away from the institutional church-es of your past. I get it. You have also taken a red pill or two. Let me encourage you to remain hopeful for what God can and will do through his people. The church exists for a reason, and our willingness to live in community with other Christians enables the best life we can experience this side of heaven. There's a church somewhere that needs you. There are people there who can help you swallow those pills—likely a couple who have taken similar pills themselves already. You don't have to worship at a "brick and mortar" and you don't have to buy into the politics of an institu-tion (not every church functions this way). Find a small group. Join a house church. But don't go it alone. There are plenty of us who are disillusioned, confused, even angry because of red pills the church has presented to us in the past. If these are your ranks, you are not alone. I'm sorry for whatever happened. I'm sorry for how you were treated. I'm sorry if someone lied to you or took advantage of you or did something hurtful to a family member. I'm sorry if you got to the point where you felt like church was just a big show put on by phonies who live secret lifestyles that rival your pagan neighbors and coworkers. You may have experienced any or all these things. All red pill awakenings. All hard to swal-low. I promise you, not every church functions this way. We need you back. We need to hear your story. We need you to share your red pills with the rest of us so we can look reality in the face and find ways to be better. That's' right, *better*. Not bitter. There's a big difference. Regardless your past experiences, *you also* need to get better. Without the help of a supportive community, you run the risk of being bitter.

So, what to do with all this? Maybe this conversation about blue and red pills can be helpful to the members of your small group. Maybe there is a discussion prompt somewhere in the paragraphs above that can trigger some meaningful conversa-tion. Maybe this is a topic to discuss with a friend at Starbucks. Consider the following: What are some of the red pills you have taken in life? Are there red pills associated with your experience of churches or the people who lead them? What are some blue pills you wish you could take again that would allow a return to a place of innocence and naivete? I wish we could sit down over coffee and discuss all this together. I would love to hear your thoughts and learn from your experiences. Chances are, there is someone near you who would gladly sit in my place. Whatever you do, please don't isolate yourself. Remember, there's a difference between bitter and better. You and I both need to get *better*. There are people somewhere right now who would love to hear your story. Sharing your red pill moments can be freeing, healing, even beneficial to others in return. You are not the only one to take a red pill, or two, or ten, or ten thousand. This is something I have learned about red pills. We all have our red pill moments, our red pill awakenings. May we seek God in all of these, even when they hurt, and confuse, and madden, and disillusion us for a season. May we learn, grow, and heal. May we become better, not bitter. May our experiences benefit others and our churches become healthier as we share our red pill revelations together in caring and supportive communities. May we be a red pill people who can discern and speak truth, who can recognize reality for what it is and meet it head on, for the blessing of others and the glory of God. Amen.

DISCUSSION 8

Text—Psalm 13; Ecclesiastes 1–2

1. Share some red pill experiences from you own life. Who and what did they involve? How (well) did you cope? Who and what helped you through?

2. Identify some blue pills that are common in our society. Why do so many people willingly consume these pills? Do any of these pills involve the church? Explain.

3. Psalm 13 is the lament of one who has swallowed a red pill or two. What emotions do you sense in this text? What are some red pills that might lead us to similar emotions? Under what circumstances might we identify with this psalm?

4. Paraphrase this psalm in one or two sentences. What is the message here? Now imagine some of your worst red pill moments. Had you written a psalm during those experiences, how would yours compare to what David writes here?

5. Read Eccl 1–2. Identify some red pill awakenings for this writer. Are these the writings of a nihilist, a realist, or someone in despair? Explain. How do we keep our own red pill awakenings from making us jaded and bitter? Solomon maintained his faith and commitment to God despite the pills he encountered. How do we maintain ours?

6. Are there red pills in your life currently that you are struggling to choke down? Are there people you need to forgive? Is it time to confide in a trusted friend or see a counselor? What about pills from your past whose bitter taste lingers on your tongue? Have you identified steps toward healing and hope? Maybe God led you to this chapter for a reason.

7. Imagine a church in which red pills were identified and addressed in healthy ways. Imagine a people who were open and honest and vulnerable, willing to share about their hurts and disappointments, knowing they would find hope and healing, comfort, and support. Imagine a church like this. Would this type of church appeal to you? Would a church like this bring hope and healing to others? Is a church like this possible?

9. Cheers

"ROVER, WANDERER, NOMAD, VAGABOND—CALL me what you will."[1] Lovers of fine poetry are likely familiar with these words from Hetfield and Ulrich. Fans of metal recognize them immediately. The song "Wherever I May Roam" was released in 1991 by the greatest band of all time, Metallica. (I know, you thought Van Halen was the greatest band of all time. Sorry to disappoint you.) The lament of this song is the hollow and superficial nature of transience for those whose work carries them from place to place, without ever finding a place to settle down, to settle in, to know others and be known in return. Those who roam never really have a home. How's that for a summary? Maybe I should write song lyrics . . .

I woke up thinking about these words today. Last night I attended a charity event to raise funds for a scholarship created in honor of my lifelong friend, Nick Petersen. Nick and I grew up together. I met Nick in the third grade, and we quickly became best friends. In the years to follow, we were baptized together, graduated high school and attended college together, served in each other's weddings, and shared what Anne of Green Gables would call a "kindred spirit" that made our friendship unique. (Yes, I'm two paragraphs in and I've already quoted James Hetfield and Anne of Green Gables. I've always been something of a Renaissance man.) In college, Nick was diagnosed with cancer. We walked this path

---

1. Metallica, "Wherever I May Roam," written by James Hetfield and Lars Ulrich, recorded in 1991, Elektra, 1992.

together. Nick was too stubborn to let a little thing like cancer beat him. Not only did Nick recover, but he also found a deeper faith, an amazing wife, and a calling to work with teenagers in his years of remission. Cancer never did get him. Complications from cancer eventually did. Nick called days before he passed to tell me he was "about to go see Jesus." Sure enough, he did. Nick was a friend, husband, coach, teacher, encourager, and evangelist—not to mention a huge fan of the Denver Broncos. Nick passed away in 2021. I spoke at that funeral.

I miss Nick and I look forward to seeing him again one day. The event I attended last night brought dozens of people together who all feel the same way. Together, we mourn, reflect, laugh, and hope. In the process, we reconnect. Growing up, Nick and I spent many hours in each other's homes. I even lived with Nick the summer before our senior year, my first (and best) experience of having a roommate. Nick's family became my family. Since Nick's passing, I've had the opportunity to reconnect with Nels and Kathy, Addi, Carrie, and Cole. I've met new spouses and all the kids. I was even honored to baptize Addi's son Caden earlier this year. When I walked in for the fundraiser event last night, I was greeted by family. I love these people and they love me. I'm thankful to be reconnected, and I'm thankful to finally live close enough to attend events like these with *family*.

We moved to Colorado Springs earlier this year for a variety of reasons. I won't get into all these here, but two are particularly relevant. First, Nick's passing had a profound affect on me. Since that funeral in 2021, I have reconnected with family and friends, some of whom I hadn't seen in over twenty years. I've been reminded of our shared experiences and encouraged by our mutual narratives. It's been a long time since I've lived in proximity to a people with whom I share a common place and history. Through all the transitions, all the moves, all the madness of life, I had somehow become unaware of how much this means to me. As a professional minister, I have uprooted my own family multiple times for the sake of churches whose members take all this for granted. My work has been to deepen relationships among people who have typically been rooted (more or less) in *their* place, and among *their* people, long before I arrived on the scene. My job has been to serve others who enjoy long standing relationships in their native habitats while my family lived as aliens. Without a place or people. Ask any of my kids where they are from or where they consider home. My children don't have memories of a place or people that make them feel at home. Our family has roamed. I regret this.

Second, and largely related to point one above, my wife and I have never involved ourselves with a church in which I wasn't a hired hand. (Minter Lane is the one exception during our ACU years. We are forever thankful for you.) The life of a professional minister is often transient. There are some out there who find a way to work with one church for ten years or more. These are the minority, and most of these relocate eventually as well (either by choice or necessity). Typically, those in paid ministry move around a bit. This is just how it works. Church work is a profession that necessitates relocation when one transitions from one employer to the next. Talk to a lifelong professional minister and you will likely hear about a variety of cities, states, even *continents* in which they have lived and worked. Such is the nature of this profession. Such is the challenge for *our* people—the ones in our homes.

Hired hands are never really *members* of their churches in quite the same way as their congregants. Our work with churches is seasonal, and our relationships are often contingent upon a paycheck. I hate to break it to you, but we are the ones who sometimes attend weddings and funerals, student events and school functions, because we are paid to be there. This goes for Sunday mornings too. Paid staff are expected to attend and participate and smile and shake hands and do all the things that make other people happy with their job performance and committed to their continued employment. We are paid to be there. Please understand, this does not make us terrible people. Most of us do care about you, and in most cases, we do the same churchy things you do with good hearts and positive intentions. Our relationship to the church is just different in some ways. We are literally paid to be there. Without the contractual obligations, our relationships might function differently. (Quick aside. Ask a paid minister if they would choose to participate with their employing church if they weren't on the payroll. They probably can't answer you honestly. In a room full of professional ministers, this is an interesting exercise. I've been in those conversations. The answers are not always encouraging.)

I've done some speaking and teaching here are there these past few years. I've traveled to a few places and met lots of great people. Of all the churches I've encountered, I was particularly impressed with the culture and leadership, the ethos, of our current church family here in Colorado Springs. I had been here twice to conduct workshops and had great experiences both times. People were kind and welcoming. Church leaders cared deeply about their young people. Elders, staff, parents, and all the golden oldies welcomed me with greater joy and authenticity than I've seen in a church for quite some time. When the time came to start a new chapter in our lives, without a clear destination in mind, and without a paid church job on my radar, we decided to move somewhere that would get us closer to a healthy and welcoming church. When people at our church ask what brought us to Colorado Springs, I tell them—*you did.* I'm not paid to attend your functions, and I might not even be there when you think I should. This time around, we are (slowly and carefully) plugging in with a church for a different set of reasons. We *choose* to be here, and we hope this enables a qualitatively different relationship with our local congregation. This time we belong as (somewhat) normal people who aren't on the payroll and have no contractual obligation to fulfill.

Earlier this year, our family enjoyed a quick trip to Boston, Massachusetts. One of the highlights from our experience was an overpriced lunch in an overcrowded restaurant known as Cheers. Caryn and I grew up watching *Cheers,* and like most eighties children (and adults and grandparents), we remember the theme song well. "Sometimes you wanna go where everybody knows your name, and they're always glad you came . . . You wanna be where everybody knows your name."[2] Many of you hummed along as you

2. Gary Portnoy, "Where Everybody Knows Your Name," written by Gary Portnoy and Judy Hart-Angelo, recorded in 1982, Applause, 1983.

read that last bit. Some of you smiled. Those lyrics brought back memories for you too, and maybe even caused you a warm fuzzy. There's a reason for this. We all resonate with those words. *Who doesn't want a place that feels like home among a people with whom you belong?* Every one of us desires these things to some degree. You can pretend that you're a loner and that you're good with it. Rover, wanderer, nomad, vagabond? Is that really what you want out of life? We all know you're lying. Deep down, you would love a Cheers community just like the rest of us.

I've been longing for a Cheers community for many years. I realize this is a romantic ideal; an unattainable reality for some. I may never find a place and people that welcome me and know my name in quite the same way as Sam and Norm and Cliff and Carla in that place called Cheers on Thursday night television. This world is not my home—I get it. But for now, I am here, in a real place and time, surrounded for better and worse by other humans who are also searching for a place and people with whom to belong, where other people know their name. In my adult years, I have largely been without these things. This is tragically ironic. As a professional minister, these are things I have worked hard to provide for others throughout my career—investing time and space with meaning, deepening and broadening relationships for others, while my family lived as aliens through our shared experience as outsiders. People knew our names for a season. People welcomed me as a hired hand—just like the guy before me, and in the same way they welcomed the guy who followed. That's not to say people were unkind. I'm painting with broad strokes here to make a point. There have always been some who welcomed and included our family. There have always been some who tried to make us feel included. What I'm describing here is simply the plight of a professional minister; the life of a ministry family that is without a place and people to ever call their own.

So, here's the deal. If you are a longtimer in your place, surrounded by your people of many years—praise God and be thankful for this. Maybe you have decades-old relationships with people who attended the same elementary school way back when. Maybe even the same prom, or college, or maybe you even worked for the same employers along the way. Maybe you are raising your kids alongside people you knew in high school. Maybe their kids will date and/or marry your kids and maybe you have even talked about this already with your spouse who is "not from here"—meaning he or she grew up thirty minutes away. Maybe your family has lived in the same town for two or three or six or ten generations and you are related to every third person you see at Walmart. Maybe your family built the church building in which you worship and your granddaddy was an elder and your daddy was an elder and you will one day be an elder and on and on. Surely, you enjoy common allegiance to the same local sports teams, know where all the obscure towns and attractions are within a certain radius of your town, can remember when this or that local restaurant closed, and know which other cities and states you are supposed to make fun of as weirdos and losers. You know all this because you are rooted. Some of you, quite deeply. You have a place and people where others know your name and they are (sometimes) glad you came—as if you ever had anywhere else to go in the first place. Rejoice and be glad. These are blessings that many will never know.

But please be careful, friends. Among you are roamers, wanderers, nomads, and vagabonds. You may not see them right away, and you may not be very welcoming when they cross your path. These are the ones you did not grow up with. These are the people with out-of-state plates on their vehicles, wearing T-shirts that support other college football teams. You may hear an unusual accent or dialect. You may wonder why they wear shorts in the "winter" or hoodies in the "summer" or think your bland foods are spicy or your spicy foods are bland. "But wait," you say. "We all cheer for this or that team here and we all like spicy or not spicy and we all know our state looks like a mitten and we all remember the Alamo and we all wear ridiculous corsages at homecoming and we all fish and hunt and we all love weekends on the lake and we all send our kids to this college or that and we all think that anyone who disagrees on these points is either ignorant or a weirdo, and we cannot tolerate different views or preferences or lifestyles or even imagine a divergent reality in which any of these things differ for others anywhere in the universe." This is only a slight exaggeration of comments I have heard and experiences I've had as an outsider in every city and state I have lived—and in every *church* I have served along the way. I hate to break it to you friends, but you may have a Cheers community that is less than cheery to outsiders. Your church may function as a social club with exclusive access to insiders and locals and homers. You may have already learned all the names you really want to know, and you might be more comfortable with this than you are willing to admit. This is an unfortunate reality for some of our churches. This might be the reality at *your* place and among *your* people.

So, here's something to consider. At your place, with your people, specifically *with your church*—if you feel like everyone knows your name and you know all of theirs, I strongly suspect there is a nomad or vagabond there somewhere among you that is yet to be seen or known or welcomed by name into a community of genuine support and meaningful belonging. When you text "everyone" to remind them of the next event at your church, you are likely missing someone. When you think you've invited "everyone" to the baby shower or the ladies' day or the golf trip or the Super Bowl party, please think again. There's a good chance someone didn't get that text. There's even a possibility someone overheard you and all your friends talking about all this in your place among your people as they waited with hope to be welcomed, invited, and included with you. Are you sure you invited *everyone*?

Last night I enjoyed a deeply meaningful experience with my people, in my place. It's good to be home after all these years—at least "home" as much as any place can be on this side of heaven. We wore our Broncos gear and talked about mountain destinations with which I was familiar. We discussed differences between the subcultures of northern and southern Colorado and compared notes on which roads and highways we prefer when traveling between the two. I've been to all these places—I'm from here, after all. The food we shared was seasoned "normally" to my taste and the social dynamics felt natural all around. Some of these people were fellow alumni of my high school, whether I knew them back then or not. Others have been friends since elementary school. For the first time in a long time, I felt at home last night—in my place and among my people. Not everyone knew my name. I'm not sure everyone was glad I came. But I do know I was there for the right reasons, with people who can take or leave me however they like without obligation and void of any pretense. This is a welcome change of pace from the life I used to live in professional ministry. No more roving and wandering for me. I'm tired of being a nomad and vagabond. I need a place and people. I need to share my experiences with my people here and do my part to make sure we see and welcome and invite and involve the wanderers in our midst, here at our place. May this be our collective endeavor, friends. May we see the wanderers among us and do everything in our power to welcome them into a place, amongst a people, where they may find deep and meaningful belonging. May we welcome others home, this side of heaven.

DISCUSSION 9

Text—Colossians 4:5–6; James 2:1–13; 1 Peter 2:9–12

1. Describe a time, place, and circumstance in which you were an outsider. Who were the insiders here? What was their commonality? How were you treated here?

2. When and where have you been an insider? What characteristics would define an outsider in these settings? Have you ever considered how new or different people might experience you and your people in this context?

3. How does 1 Pet 2:9–12 describe the people of God in relation to the rest of the world? To what extent do we find a Cheers community here? Is this community intended to be exclusive? Explain.

4. Read Col 4:5–6. Paul makes a distinction here between insiders and outsiders. How should Christians relate to people who have not accepted Christ as Lord? List some practical examples of Christ followers "making the most of every opportunity" to show and share Jesus with others in our own place and time. Do we actively seek these opportunities? Do we pray for God to put us in places with people who need Jesus? Why or why not?

5. James 2:1–13 acknowledges the human tendency to treat people differently based on superficial matters. Have you experienced churches who treat wealthy people as insiders and less wealthy people as something different? Have you seen similar principles among natives and foreigners; family clans and transplants? In your experience, to what extent do churches show favoritism on matters of age, race, gender, and socioeconomic status today?

6. How do you think non-Christians view most churches today? Are churches like country clubs, in which certain people can be members, paying dues and gaining access to exclusive privileges? Are churches political organizations in which members vote and picket and protest and consume shared narratives from agreed-upon news outlets? Are churches safe and welcoming places for people who look or feel different—people whose lives are not perfect?

7. Imagine a church in which everyone knew your name. Now imagine that others in this church shared the same experience. Imagine a group of people who refused to let anyone be an outsider, a group committed to learning names and faces and hearing the stories of everyone they encountered. Imagine if this church extended beyond the confines of any building, with the desire to know and involve and include neighbors and co-workers and classmates as part of a community of mutual support and shared concern. Can you imagine a church like this?

10. Maps: Part 1

MY SON AND I listened to the Wiggles on our drive to school this morning (much to his dismay). I have three or four of their hits in my playlist, and I genuinely enjoy these songs. As kids' music goes, I think the Wiggles are top notch. Of course, I only know these songs because I raised children in the early 2000s. My daughter and I attended a Wiggles concert in Portland, Oregon, back when she was a toddler. I have great memories of this experience. This is the actual reason the Wiggles remain in my playlist today.

Not included on my playlist is another song I remember vividly from this era. Parents of my age and kids who grew up during that time got their fair share of *Dora the Explorer*. This was a television show about a little girl who traveled and explored with an odd cast of friends—humans, animals, and inanimate objects with mouths and eyes. (Kids' television is always a bit creepy if you think about it.) In every episode, a time would come in which Dora couldn't find her way forward. At this time, Dora would consult her trusty friend, the Map. (Clever, right?) The Map had a theme song that some of you remember well. *"I'm the map, I'm the map, I'm the map . . ."* repeated indefinitely until the Map finally provided directions to Dora and her crew. Without the Map, Dora would never have found her way.

I write this chapter at the request of a friend. This two-part chapter is the last in a series of blog posts that make up this book. I began writing as an experiment, curious to see if any would resonate with my take on a variety of things that keep me awake at night. The results were mixed. Three or four read and responded privately with every post. A handful of others have offered financial sponsorship for this project (you know who you are—thank you). Far more clicked the links, but I have no way to know if they read beyond random titles and silly introductions about childhood television series. Analytics provided by my blogging platform suggest more readers than I anticipated. I'm not sure what to do with all this. I have prayed from the beginning that these essays would find their way to the people (and churches) who needed them most. Hopefully, this has happened—whether I ever know it or not.

When discussing how to close this series, a friend suggested something practical that would move from the observations and insights of previous entries toward creative and practical solutions in my final installment. My friend suggested a "map" of sorts for my readers. "Why don't you share some things the church will need to recognize and address to survive and thrive in the future? Give us some ideas of how to do things differently, that might be more healthy, effective, or practical for our people. Times have changed, our culture is evolving rapidly, and our churches are often without a clue how to survive, let alone thrive, amid conflict, confusion, and widespread complacency." (This is more or less the quote—you get the idea.) Toward this end, I conclude this series with a map. I've divided this entry into two pieces for the sake of my readers. If you don't hate this first part, maybe you will also consider reading part two.

Maps are tools that help us find our way from one place to another. In many cases, maps are elective resources. Some people have a great sense of direction; others simply enjoy explorative approaches to wayfinding. For those who appreciate something tangible to consult along the way, maps bring clarity to our starting and ending points, helping travelers identify and navigate the space between. The map that follows is my feeble attempt to identify some turning points in the road ahead as our churches navigate a challenging path forward. You can take or leave any of this without hurting my feelings. I pray there is something here that will benefit you and your people to the glory of God, for the strengthening, deepening, and broadening of his kingdom this side of heaven.

Journeys begin with a starting point. The first thing to do when consulting a map is to identify our place of origin. I write today from Colorado Springs. Wherever I may travel from here will require me to first find Colorado Springs on the map to determine its directional proximity to the place I am planning to go. Once determined, I can locate the place of my intended destination and begin charting a course from here to there. Denver is North. Albuquerque is South. In each case, my starting place is the same. Effective map reading begins with locating our starting point. Only after this point is clearly established can we begin to chart the path forward.

The map for our churches begins with a current starting point called *More Is Less*. This is where we are in North American Protestantism at the time of this writing. More Is Less. Think about this for a moment. How do churches measure their impact in 2023? To varying degrees, this sort of thing usually has something to do with more people in attendance at our gatherings, more money in our offering plates, more professional staff to coordinate our programming, more programming to fill our calendars, more buildings to facilitate our programs, and more campuses in our satellite networks—all so we can do more of these things in more places, which inevitably requires even more staffing, programming, and funding. More, more, more.

Our intentions here are mixed. For some these are good. We desire to reach the lost and nurture the saved. We want a larger footprint as we claim a fallen world back for the purposes of God. I can get behind most of that, I think. In other cases, we simply want more because we are prideful and egotistical people; some of us narcissists who crave power and attention and money and pictures of our faces and buildings and corporate logos smattered among billboards, book covers, and posters for Christian conferences of all kinds. Don't be naive, friends. There are plenty of reasons our churches and their leaders embrace More Is Less—not all of which are noble.

I know—your church is nothing like this. I get it. My church is not like this either. That said, I suspect your church and mine (and the others on your block and across the street from yours and mine) share some common assumptions and practices that locate us squarely in the community of More Is Less. Never mind the extreme versions of mega this or that in the surrounding community of More Is Less. Think about *your* church. Be honest. *Where do you meet?* What does it cost to pay the mortgage and utility bills for your facility every month? How do you finance a broken furnace or air conditioning unit when these things inevitably occur? *Who spearheads your programming?* In other words, who do you pay to lead the various ministries of your church? How many of these people are on your staff? (It's a good bet that facility costs and staff salaries constitute the majority of your church budget. Don't believe me? When is the last time you looked at the numbers for yourself?) *How central are "tithes and offerings" to the operational language of your congregation?* Have you ever wondered why we give so much attention to financial offerings in the context of our worship assemblies? We do this because we need money to fund our facility maintenance and professional staff. Without these things it is much harder to facilitate programming that is desirable and competitive amidst the vast offerings of other churches in our More Is Less community.

More Is Less. Many of our churches have become fat, lazy, and entitled. Decades of cultural acceptance (toleration, at least) have enabled us to enjoy a mainstream presence with "big box" church buildings sprinkled among big box retailers—often with little distinction. We've bought land, built huge structures, and paved expansive parking lots a la Best Buy and Hobby Lobby. We cannot imagine churches without church *buildings*. We've become fat. These facilities are empty most of the week and increasingly empty on Sunday mornings. Church buildings may be luxuries of the past we simply cannot afford in the future. We have purchased and accumulated and acquired—and become fat.

Likewise, we have hired increasingly more *paid professionals* to facilitate the programs of our churches. I grew up with a solitary preacher in my church. As a ministry professional, I've been surrounded by youth, children's, family, worship, education, executive, and even some technology and A/V ministers—all paid staffers—for many years. We have so over-professionalized the field of ministry that we truly believe we need professionals in all these areas to facilitate the programs of our churches. Want something done at your church? Pay someone to do it. Let's be clear: if your sermons are scheduled and timed and evaluated by church leaders, even these constitute a program for your church. You likely pay someone to present content for 22.5 minutes every Sunday at 10:48 a.m. (assuming you are on schedule based on the parameters created by your worship minister). Preaching is often a program, almost always conducted by a paid professional. No need for members of our churches to present from the front of the room. They may stutter or go too long or say too little or lack a funny story or be the wrong gender or age or be less inviting to seekers who evaluate our church based on societal expectations for professional orators. We hire professionals for such things. We've become lazy.

In the end, we have invested fully into a church culture that exists to provide goods and services to consumers who have a plethora of options from which to choose in the More Is Less Christian community. We hire people to create programs to attract consumers (and retain current attendees) who are shopping for the best events and the coolest T-shirts and the most exotic mission trip experiences and the most dynamic presentations and the most experiential worship offerings, and, and, and. We know that if we do not provide these things, we will not be attractive to outsiders or able to fully retain our insiders (who also know other churches in the area have all these things in greater number and with more dynamism and maybe suited more to their tastes and preferences). We've become entitled. We want more from our churches, but often more of very little that will nurture us to become more like Jesus in our attempt to follow him. Years of accumulating and acquiring *more* has not led to more spiritually mature churches. We've known for a long time that teenagers walk away from their churches after high school graduation. This, despite the most well-resourced industry and über professionalized youth ministry programs our world has ever seen. More facilities, increased funding, and increasingly professionalized staffing for our student ministry programs has *not* led to more and deeper Christians carrying our flag forward for future generations of Christ followers. We've invested *more* of all these things and the result has been *less* than what we ever hoped for. As children's ministry becomes more professionalized, we will likely achieve the same results. More staff members to lead more programs to achieve less for the kingdom when all is said and done. Sorry, friends. Our starting point on the map as we look desperately for a path forward begins with More Is Less. We are a fat, lazy, and entitled people. We live in a place called *More Is Less*. From here we begin our journey forward . . .

DISCUSSION 10

Text—Acts 2:42–47; 4:32–35; 1 Corinthians 14:26

1. What is your initial response to this chapter? The author claims that many churches today are fat, lazy, and entitled. Ouch! Is this a fair assessment? Explain.

2. How would you describe "church" to someone unfamiliar with this concept? Provide your best explanations of who, what, when, where, why, and how as these pertain to the topic.

3. Read the above passages from Acts. Here we find snapshots of the earliest church and her defining features. Revisit question 2 above. How would we describe "church" for the earliest Christians, based upon these passages?

4. Read 1 Cor 14:26. How do we interpret and apply this passage to our contemporary worship gatherings? Does this verse merely describe an early worship assembly, or does it prescribe a format for worship gatherings then and now? Explain.

5. Compare your experience of contemporary churches with what we find in the passages above. Who does what, when, where, why, and how? Should we consider biblical precedents as normative examples of how the church should look and function today? Explain.

6. Notice what is lacking in all the above passages. What role should programs, presentations, and paid professionals have in our churches today? To what extent should we prioritize buildings and budgets as central to achieving our purpose? Is there actual danger that all these can make our churches fat, lazy, and entitled?

7. Imagine a church in which More Is Less has little intrigue. Imagine a people gathered around a common commitment to Christ, with little concern for building renovations, budget campaigns, or butts-in-seats as markers of dynamism in the Christian marketplace. Imagine a church like this. What is necessary to cultivate and nurture a church like this today?

11. Maps: Part 2

Having found our starting point at *More Is Less*, we next pinpoint our destination. In the case of our churches, this is a place we need to find whether we like it or not. Moving forward, churches and their leaders will need to embrace the reality that More Is Less has never been the utopia we have imagined. Others have been vacating More Is Less for years. The population is steadily shrinking. More Is Less has a leaky roof and a shrinking budget to fund her repair. More Is Less has fewer professionals to lead her programs. More Is Less has been tried and found wanting. Turns out, more of this and that here and there has not resulted in more faith, more committed Christ followers, or more meaningful and lasting impact for God's kingdom. *More has been less for quite some time now.* So, we move. We must. We begin a journey from More Is Less to *Less Is More*. This is the new (old) horizon for our churches—the place to which we journey as we make our home this side of heaven.

Less Is More holds to a different set of ideals. There is a different culture and ethos in this community, one in which facilities, budgets, programs, and paid professionals are not *evil*, but simply not upheld as *essential* resources for God's people. As new as this idea may be to some readers, I believe it is a more accurate depiction of the church as presented in the New Testament. The earliest churches had few of the comforts we enjoy today, yet they loved and cared for one another; they grew in number and spread like wildfire in a hostile environment. Churches gathered and worshiped and shared communion and pooled resources to pay for others' needs. Churches enfolded new converts while older people mentored younger people and parents trained up their children without a paid minister or VBS or church camp or mission trip experience. Somehow, generations of Christians resulted without implement of professionalized ministry programs. Paul encouraged his churches to be generous, and even told them to set aside money for regular collections. As far as I can tell, this was never to pay for a broken air conditioner in the church gymnasium or to finance the repaving of a cracked and faded church parking lot. Who knows? Maybe Paul envisioned a paid worship minister to set parameters for the length and content of his sermons. Maybe an executive minister to hire and fire staff with the aid of a human resources professional (yes, these are actual paid positions in some of our churches today). Maybe the goal was to provide a multimillion-dollar, state-of-the-art facility in which to host Tim Tebow and the stars of *Duck Dynasty* for their respective events and conferences. I suppose that may have been his vision for the future of God's churches. *More of this and that.*

I suspect not. Consider the following as a poignant contrast between the communities of More Is Less and Less Is More. I went to a church in college that boasted about how quickly they could serve communion to a gathering of almost two thousand people every Sunday. This took a coordinated effort to be sure. Imagine what it takes to knock out communion (including the financial offering that is typically included here, though very much "separate and apart from" the Lord's Supper) with that many people in just a few minutes! Here we see More Is Less clearly at work in a well-intentioned church full of good people who really thought they were doing things to honor God by doing them in an orderly fashion. True! And sadly, false. In this case, more people at the gathering required more efficiency to be served—in the shortest and most impersonal way possible. Post-COVID, most churches have the added luxury of self-serve rip-and-sip communion kits that people can pick up at the doors and dispose of immediately. No longer do we need servers at all. Imagine the gains in efficiency, particularly with our larger churches. Today, we have no reason for the weekly communion time to extend past two or three minutes. This leaves more time for sermons, collections, and our favorite worship ballads. As long as we pack all these consistently into a tight sixty minutes.

Around this same time during my college experience, I was blessed to share communion one Sunday with a group of Christians in Dresden, Germany. For me, this was an early peek at *Less Is More* as a hopeful and life-giving destination for God's people. Twenty of us gathered on that day. Communion was served by our host couple from their finest crystal. We shared glasses by necessity, as they didn't have enough to go around. The bread was freshly baked. The comments and reflections came from different voices around the room. I don't remember how long it took—because no one was trying to keep us on a fixed schedule or trying to set a record for how fast we could pass out and collect disposable plastic cups so everyone could get out on time and beat the Baptists to Applebee's. Looking back, I doubt there was a Tuesday morning staff meeting to assess the timing or quality of peoples' comments, let alone glitches with microphones or PowerPoint slides that weren't advanced properly. Maybe I am naive, but I like to think a group of Christians gathered without pretense and void of professionalism in that apartment, where nonpaid leaders offered communion and a committed group of Christ followers shared and reflected for as long as we wanted while deepening our relationships through this interactive, all-inclusive experience. This is a good example of how things function differently in the community of Less Is More. Fewer comments from a podium. Less emphasis on timing and efficiency. No need for themed presentations or printed worship orders on church bulletins (which cost our churches time and money, are rarely utilized, and get thrown away by church janitors at the close of every corporate assembly). Less of all that, but with *more impact* for all who participate.

These past couple years my college-aged children have reflected often about their experiences growing up in the various churches I served in my tenure as a paid staffer. One contrast is particularly notable. Our family has lived in a handful of places over the years. We have experienced churches of various size in some very different contexts. With size has come staff and budget and programs and all sorts of things that the smaller churches in our past could not afford. In one case, I served a church with multiple children's ministers. This church had two *wings* of our building dedicated to children's ministry. In my first year with this congregation a remodel was given to one of these wings at the cost of $150,000. This, in addition to regular expenses of staff, interns, operational expenses, camps, T-shirts, and animal rentals for seasonal on-campus petting zoos (we literally provided pony rides). Our teaching materials were developed in-house around themed classrooms that rivaled Disney properties, and our Sunday morning classes required almost fifty volunteers to run smoothly. Think about all that for a moment. More of everything, from my own life experience. Plenty more of this and that and the other.

Contrast this with a little church I served in a suburb of Detroit, Michigan. In this church, we had no paid staffers to lead our children's ministry. Technically, we had no "children's ministry" at all. What we did have were two ladies who taught a Wednesday night Bible class for the children of our congregation. There were several weeks when my kids were the only ones in attendance. Diane and Rosemary taught faithfully for years, without any budget, without themed classrooms, without any bells or whistles or T-shirts or pony rides. Ask my kids where they learned more about the Bible. Ask them where they saw Jesus modeled by people who knew them personally and loved them deeply. Ask where they weren't a number to be counted or a consumer to be placated. Each of my grown children will tell you they learned more about Jesus from those two ladies on Wednesday nights in a stale and boring classroom where they were sometimes the only children in attendance. Hands down. This is an excellent example of life in *Less Is More*. Nurturing the faith of our littles is less complicated than we make it out to be. We don't need the dog and pony shows. More of all that can be *less* when it comes to the long-term spiritual development of or children and teenagers. Diane and Rosemary are worth their weight in gold. The costly remodel of your children's ministry spaces is worth far less. I promise.

Less Is More doesn't require properties and facilities and buildings and parking lots. The people of Less Is More appreciate the intimacy that is found in smaller gatherings, where people know others deeply and are known deeply in return. Smaller gatherings fit in smaller places. Churches in More Is Less become enamored with building projects and facility expansions. How many we can *fit* becomes more important than how many we can *know*. Your auditorium may seat five hundred, but I doubt you've ever seen it full. What's the point? What purpose does all this space serve? (And how much does it cost to heat and cool it with the changing seasons?) Assuming you can gather three hundred in that space, how many know others deeply based on shared experiences in this room? Expand this principle to include your classroom space, gymnasium, multipurpose spaces, parking areas, church grounds, and surrounding acreage. Maybe you build relationships better in these adjacent spaces, but how much does it cost to maintain them? We encounter multiple challenges here. Hear me plainly. Our churches enjoyed a season of *feasting*, in which we accumulated and acquired. *Buildings and grounds are what we have to show for our efforts.* The time has come for *fasting*. There is nothing wrong with buildings and grounds and campuses and acreages and parsonages-turned-youth houses. Unfortunately, it is time to recognize these things for what they are. Investments in structures and real estate that have little to do with discipleship and kingdom impact this side of heaven. We must reconceive our operations as we enter a season of fasting. We must recognize that we never really needed all the buildings and grounds and mortgages and plumbing repairs and grass cutting and snow removal services first place. More has been less for a long, long time.

Less Is More prioritizes people over places. Relationships are more important here, and relationships are nurtured in smaller, more intimate environments. As we navigate from More Is Less to Less Is More, some of our churches will need to repurpose and/or sell some of our facilities. We no longer fill the places we have built, and we have never fully utilized these spaces for consistent and meaningful use to begin with. For churches that cling to underutilized facilities, we need to think creatively about ways to repurpose these spaces to provide income to finance their maintenance or to provide spaces for people to work and live who are without options elsewhere. Either rent out your space for offices during the week or convert it into free and low-income housing for people in need. If you pay to condition the air in these facilities, there had better be a reason. If you insist on paying a full staff of age and ministry specific professional staffers at your place, maybe converting a few classrooms into rentable offices for local businesses will generate some income to pay these salaries. *Those rooms are vacant most of the time.* Either utilize them to a fuller purpose or be done with them entirely. The age of big box church buildings is ending. It's time we learn to do with fewer and smaller facilities. It's time to move our gatherings from large auditoriums to kitchens and living rooms and backyards with people on our decks gathered around smoking barbecue grills. Relationships are built in places like these. Worship of all kinds happens here. Everyone is included, regardless of age or gender. Pay someone to preach here if you like, but I'm not sure this is necessary. Less Is More.

Less Is More is populated and led by invested citizens who live here knowing they must be actively involved for the community to exist in its fullness. The people of Less Is More contribute to the life of their churches with more than tithes and offerings. Remember that church that needed fifty volunteers to facilitate their children's classes every Sunday morning? The greatest challenge for our paid staffers in that department was recruiting and retaining said volunteers for this purpose. When we pay people to lead programs, we tend to assume those bases are covered without any additional help required. Why should you or I volunteer to do something we already pay someone else to do? This is very much our thinking with professional youth (and children's) ministry. Have Bible studies with my teenager? We have a guy (or girl) on staff who is paid to do this. Churches have gotten into the habit of outsourcing spiritual formation to paid professionals, assuming the church provides necessary resources for all this by way of our tithes and offerings. We pay professionals to provide these services. Be honest, friends. How well has all this worked out for our churches, for your own grown children?

Less paid staff with less programming. Really? This would require moms and dads to play an active role in the spiritual development of their children and teenagers. Parents initiating Bible studies, serving alongside their children in the community, making visits to hospitals and pilgrimages to children's homes without paid professionals to coordinate all these activities. Families may need to open their homes for ministry with the friends of their children. Parents may need to meet other parents and begin spiritual conversations outside of church buildings and with greater aims than simply inviting others to church—where paid professionals can take the handoff and begin the *real* work of ministry. Less Is More values invitations to backyard barbecues for neighbors and coworkers and the classmates of our children. I have a good friend in the Pacific Northwest who leads a youth group that evolved organically from the peer gatherings of his teenage son. There is no paid youth worker in this congregation. No calendar of programs. No youth budget to fund events or T-shirts. This church has a family that is willing to host their kids' friends at any time and for any reason, with hope that they may share Jesus in the process. Less Is More.

I have plenty of friends in professional ministry. Indeed, this has been my own industry for many years. Please understand—I have no interest in discrediting my peers, nor do I want to hurt them in any way here. I do believe more will need to become bivocational and many will need to minister without pay as churches tighten their belts in the years to come. That said, paid staffers can absolutely add value to the life and practices of your congregation. I am a big fan of youth pastors, in particular—assuming they approach their task as bridge builders between Jesus, teenagers, and adults of all ages. Believe it or not, this can be done on a tight budget and without fanfare. (No need for dog and pony shows.) There are ways to do youth ministry well, that sometimes benefit from paid professionals to lead the charge. But let's be clear. Paid staffers in roles like these are luxuries we have enjoyed in years of feasting—common features of churches that became fat, lazy, and entitled somewhere along the way. In the *fasting* season to come, churches will be stripped of luxuries like these, forced to identify what is truly necessary for the health and vitality of their people. The good news is that God ordained *families* to nurture the faith of our young people as far back as the time of Moses. Our churches have untapped internal resources to provide what our children, and their friends, and their friends' parents need when it comes to showing and sharing Jesus. We are capable of more than we realize when we don't outsource spiritual formation, education, and evangelism to the professionals.

I've promised to be honest from the beginning of this book. I've promised to tell the truth, whether you agree, whether you like it or not. The truth is I have enjoyed a professional career as a paid staffer in local churches for over twenty years. I hold graduate and doctoral degrees in theology and ministry. I've worked as a youth pastor all this time and have been compensated well. At various times, I have enjoyed salary packages worth $80–90K with insurance and benefits. Every church I've served has been generous with vacation time. I've been blessed to own a house everywhere we've lived. Some of my churches have provided professional opportunities and personal connections enabling me to speak at conferences and rub shoulders with other ministers whose names you know. At one point, my professional employment with a particular congregation served as catalyst for my receipt of an alumni award from my alma mater. I know this because I've learned more about the politics of churches and their network of related colleges and universities through my tenure in professional ministry. I have benefitted from this system.

I have also seen behind the curtain. I have participated in many elder and minister meetings over the years. I've been in those Tuesday morning staff meetings where we critique our Sunday worship service, everything from content to delivery and even "production value" as stated by one colleague a few years back. I've also been in the budget planning sessions. I know about years of feasting and years of famine, and I've seen firsthand the implications for the budgets and staff and programs and facilities and missionaries and kingdom impact of our churches. I understand the delicate balance between pleasing insiders and attracting outsiders when it comes to how we spend our time and money. I realize that we choose our battles based on comfort and preference more often than for theological conviction or any real sense of concern for a fallen world that is going to hell. People like me get paid—sometimes quite well—to manage all these things in the trenches of professional ministry. I suppose I've never done this very well. If so, I might have a professional career with a fancy title at a well-paying church today. I could be Doctor Blanchard—I already have the diploma!

Scripture speaks of the church as the bride of Christ. In his wisdom, God created the church as a vehicle for reconciliation with a fallen world; a place to know others and be known in return, first from those who welcome us to their living rooms and kitchen tables and then from Jesus Christ himself. The church is a light to the world, a refuge for the hurting, a place of hope and healing for the fallen and afflicted. The church is filled with the Spirit of God—at least it should be. I'm not sure this has always been my experience with local churches. Some appear to have lost their way. Plenty have become fat, lazy, and entitled. *Is this how we envision the bride of Christ?* We love our places more than our people, we rely on paid professionals to do the actual work of ministry while we watch from the sidelines, and we expect churches to "meet our needs" (perceived or real), lest we take our tithes and offerings elsewhere. These are common markers of the More Is Less mentality that has infected many of our local congregations.

The time has come to journey forward to the place where Less Is More, a community in which churches meet in homes, backyards, parks, and public spaces, without all the mess and overhead that comes with buildings and grounds. The time has come to embrace a priesthood of all believers in which every person brings a talent, a word, an act of service to the gathered community as essential contributors to the common good. People of diverse age and gender and social status, with or without anyone in the mix who is paid for their service. The church was never meant to be a professional organization. The time has come to recognize that our calendars are already too busy and that it is not the job of any church to provide a full schedule of age specific programming for every season. Fewer programs require fewer staff which requires less funding and maybe even fewer facilities to heat and cool and insure. Less programming. Less paid staffers. Less building maintenance. Less concern over budgetary matters for our local congregations. Many of our churches are on the cusp of these conversations already. There are less people in their pews and less money in their offering plates. Leaders are meeting now to discuss budget shortfalls and consider additional pleas for tithes and offerings. If something doesn't change, and soon, these churches will be forced to cut programs, fire staff, and eventually liquidate some assets, *whether they like it or not*. How did we ever get here? More importantly, where do we go from here? It's time we journey forward. *More Is Less has been tried and found wanting.* Decades of feasting has made our churches fat, lazy, and entitled. In the season of fasting that is rapidly encroaching, we leave More Is Less in the rear view and begin our steady, prayerful movement toward Less Is More—our best hope for a future, a place where churches not only survive, but may even *thrive* this side of heaven.

DISCUSSION 11

Text—Deuteronomy 6:1–9; 1 Corinthians 16:19;
Colossians 4:15; 1 Peter 2:4–5; 9–12

1. Summarize and compare the defining characteristics of More Is Less and Less Is More churches. Which of these churches is most similar to those you have experienced personally?

2. Read the above passages from 1 Peter. What would our churches look like and how would they function if we lived into our identity as a priesthood of all believers? What implications would result for paid staff, ministry leaders, volunteers, golden oldies, singles, parents, teenagers, and children?

3. Deuteronomy 6 outlines God's design for the spiritual development of our young people. Has the professionalization of age-specific ministers and their related programming helped or hurt in achieving this ideal? What would our churches look like if faith was nurtured within nuclear families, supported by the larger congregation as a whole? What challenges and opportunities do you imagine here?

4. Notice Paul's comments in 1 Cor 16 and Col 4. Where did some early Christians meet for worship and fellowship? Provide examples of this happening today. What advantages and disadvantages accompany a different meeting space with a different format for worship and fellowship than what we find in "big box churches" today? Is this appealing or appalling to you? Explain.

5. Less Is More values intimacy and rejects apathy. All are welcomed and valued here. All hands are required to serve. Programs and professionals are welcome, but not necessary. Budget drives and building campaigns are not the focus here. How does this sound to you? Is this an unrealistic expectation for churches today?

6. What would it take to cultivate and nurture a Less Is More church in your context? Maybe you are part of one already. Maybe your church is huge; maybe it is small. What principles from Less Is More can be applied in your current setting? How and where do you begin? Explain.

7. Imagine a church in which Less Is More; where people know this from the deep, rich, and transformative lives they live and share together. Imagine a church where every person embraces their priestly identity and uses their God-given gifts to serve and minister to others. Imagine if parents nurtured the faith of their children, supported by the body, and without need of professionals to lead programs and activities. Imagine if this church could use all her resources to care for the needs of people, inside and out, without all her finances tied up in the mortgages and maintenance of underutilized facilities. Have you experienced a church like this before? Would you like to?

Keep the conversation going! Share this book with family, friends, or your small group. This book is intended to be discussed with others. Imagine a group of people intent on following Jesus as best they can. Imagine if this group gathered around tables, in living rooms and garages, at coffee shops and local pubs, in classrooms and auditoriums, to discuss life and faith and the church, with this little book as a conversation starter. Additional copies are available online at: www.wipfandstock.com

To schedule a speaking, teaching, or training event with the author, send an email to:
daveblanchard76@outlook.com

www.ingramcontent.com/pod-product-compliance
Lightning Source LLC
Chambersburg PA
CBHW052134090426
42741CB00009B/2075